HOW TO STOP AND INFLUENCE PLANNING PERMISSION

~

Roy Speer & Michael Dade

Published by Stonepound Books

ACKNOWLEDGEMENTS

We thank the following for their help with the book: numerous planning officers and civil servants throughout the United Kingdom for providing information; David Edmonds for the layout and cover design; Barry Page for the cover photo 'View from Clayton Hill, Hassocks'; Ivan Hissey for his cartoons; and Alan Hoskins for permission to reproduce his campaign leaflet. Special thanks to Tina, Rowan and Josie Dade, and Pennie, Emma, George and Harry Speer without whose support the book would not have been written.

NOTE

Names and other details given in some of the examples in this book are for the purpose of illustration only. No reference to real people and places is intended or should be inferred.

Third edition 2001 published by
Stonepound Books
10 Stonepound Road
Hassocks West Sussex BN6 8PP
01273 842155
www.stonepound.co.uk

First edition published 1994 by J M Dent Ltd
Second edition published 1998 by Stonepound Books
Copyright © Roy Speer and Michael Dade 2001

ISBN 0 9533489 0 3

Designed by David Edmonds Presentation, Graphics and Design
0208 295 1901
Cover photograph by Page Photographic 01273 844856
Printed and bound by XPS Limited, Brighton 01273 421242

'The only long term winners will be the developers, certainly not the town as they will have us believe. We will have lost further amounts of countryside to gain yet another stretch of concrete.'

'The latest proposals for several thousand houses in the county, much of it on greenfield sites, must inevitably impinge even further on our way of life. Can we hope for a change of heart?'

'We believe our views are important because our knowledge of the park seems to be greater than those who have the power to decide what is going to be done there. Decisions based on lack of knowledge can never be good decisions. Can our voice be heard - before it is too late to have an effect?'

These words are quotes taken from newspapers, from members of the public concerned about development. In a similar situation what would you do? Could you change anything anyway? How would you go about making your voice heard?

In the 2000s, we're much more aware of the environment - natural and built - and are more concerned about environmental issues than we were say fifteen, ten or even five years ago. Few people now are prepared to sit back and let developers and local politicians decide what's best for their communities, yet fewer still have any idea of how the planning system - the system that governs change in our towns and countryside - works and how we can influence decisions on specific development proposals. As a consequence, public participation in the planning system is under-utilised by the people it's there to serve.

But do you as an individual or group have any real power? Objectors to the proposed redevelopment of Kings Cross in London secured amendments, caused four years' delay and cost the developers an estimated £45 million. Judge for yourself. Again, controversial plans to build a four-lane trunk road through the 5 hectare (12 acre), 8,000 year-old Oxleas Wood in south London were abandoned by the government after a sustained campaign involving two public inquiries, intervention by the European Community and a series of legal challenges.

Regardless of commitments by politicians of all parties to protect the environment, substantial development, based on housing need and job creation, is still programmed. Such development, however, is planned and carried out over many years and some of it is necessary. Even though you might not be able to stop some development taking place, you can still try to influence where it will be located, what form it will take and what can be done to minimise its impact. For example:

- do you want new development to be built in the countryside or in existing towns and cities?
- do you want town centres to keep their traditional appearance or to be comprehensively redeveloped?
- do you want to see a new road go through a tunnel rather than through ancient woodland?

HOW TO STOP AND INFLUENCE PLANNING PERMISSION is a practical manual that shows you how to take effective action and participate in decisions that affect your life. It tells you what to do, where to go and who to speak to. It also discusses what arguments to use and how to set them out in objection letters and statements. This book is not anti or pro-development. Our aim is to enable you and other members of the public to influence development decisions by giving a unique insight into the planning system, based on our practical experience of its operation.

People who object to development or who want to have a say, generally aren't interested in Acts of Parliament or Statutory Instruments; rather, they want to know how to go about making their opinions count. In this guide, therefore, we explain planning procedure only to give a necessary understanding of the system you'll have to use. You can research legal and procedural detail, if that is what you want, in planning law books at libraries and book shops. Government departments, for example, produce booklets summarizing various planning procedures (see appendix II), and most are available from council offices or on the internet. All these books and booklets are useful - as far as they go - but what you need to know, if you are to change anything, are the tips that official publications don't tell you.

HOW TO STOP AND INFLUENCE PLANNING PERMISSION is based on the law in England and Wales. Although Scotland and Northern Ireland are covered by different laws, and terminology varies, their planning systems are similar to those in England and Wales. Significant differences are mentioned in the relevant sections of text. The information in this edition was correct as at spring 2001 – bear in mind that law, administration and policies change. Throughout this book, 'his/her' should be understood wherever 'his' appears since planning officers, inspectors and councillors, as well as those seeking planning permission, could equally be female or male.

Our book starts by setting out the background to the planning system and discusses the factors that influence all planning decisions (Chapter 1). If you're serious about achieving real results, it's extremely important to understand the system and its decision making basis for your actions to be truly effective. The remainder of the book guides your actions in specific situations, such as planning appeals or enforcement. No book, however, can give definitive advice on specific cases. If you're ever in any doubt, get help from the council, a professional or one of the bodies listed in the appendices.

On the whole, individual action on wider questions of national and strategic issues is less likely to be successful. These might be on the law itself, European or national policies for development, or policies for whole counties or regions. The best way that you can influence these wider issues is to join or support a national pressure group or political party.

Is the planning system so complex that you shouldn't even try to get involved? Are the odds stacked too heavily against you? No. Armed with the knowledge gained from HOW TO STOP AND INFLUENCE PLANNING PERMISSION, you can make a difference. Here are some examples of successful action:

Substantial and vigorous local opposition thwarted plans for a 50 seater McDonald's restaurant in the London Borough of Enfield. Objections focused on the effects of noise and traffic generation on a quiet residential area.

A local resident obtained a court order obliging Rochdale Council to review the conditions under which an old quarry could re-open. Working hours, site restoration plans, after use and traffic generation were among the issues the council had to reconsider.

A controversial scheme to convert a pub to residential use in Sherington, Bucks, was refused after a public inquiry. Following the decision a senior council planning officer commented: 'I believe that the strength of local opinion expressed in writing and voiced at the inquiry significantly assisted the council's case'.

The planning system is now such an established part of modern life that few people question its existence. Planning isn't new: the ancient Egyptians, Greeks, Romans, Incas and Aztecs all planned their cities. In the United Kingdom, the planning system has evolved over many years in response to the growth of population and industrialisation. Some of the finest examples of planned development are those eighteenth and nineteenth-century estates in places such as Edinburgh and Bath. These pre-date the formal planning system which was introduced in 1947, after the second World War left huge devastated areas of towns and cities to be rebuilt.

The planning system is designed to regulate development in the public interest by providing curbs on harmful development, striking a balance between conservation and exploitation of buildings and land, and reconciling private and community interests.

THE SYSTEM

Responsibility for managing the planning system is split between central and local government (see Figure 1.1). England, Northern Ireland, Scotland and Wales are administered separately. Local government in most of England comprises two layers: county councils, and district or borough councils. In English metropolitan areas, plus a few other areas in England, and throughout Scotland and Wales, there are single-tier councils, often called 'unitary authorities'. The Planning Service of the Northern Ireland Assembly administers the planning system through six divisional offices. National Parks have their own planning authorities which decide planning applications (see Chapter 6).

Councils are sometimes called 'local planning authorities'. For convenience, we use the term 'district council' throughout this book to include all councils which decide planning applications. Most district council areas are divided still further into parish, town or community councils; these we shall refer to as 'parish councils'. Parish councils are consulted and make recommendations on planning applications but have no legal power to decide them. The weight given to their views varies widely. Some parish councils have influence in practice because their recommendations are followed closely by the district council.

Although the European Union doesn't play a direct role in operating the UK planning system, one of the functions of its Commissioners is to ensure that EU directives are complied with in EU countries. This led, for example, to a ruling by the European Court that the UK government had acted illegally in leaving an area of international wildlife importance out of the Medway Estuary Special Protection Area in Kent.

Planning functions

Planning is divided into two distinct parts: forward planning and development control, and there are opportunities within both parts to bring your influence to bear. Forward planning is done by central government and local government to guide future development in an efficient and orderly way. Central government draws up national guidelines which are translated by local government into county Structure Plans and district council Local Plans or Unitary Development Plans (see page 10). Development control over individual planning proposals is operated mainly by district councils, which grant planning permission where a proposal complies with policies laid down in the forward planning documents. Some types of development known as 'permitted development' can take place without the need for planning permission (see Figures 1.2 and 1.3). In most cases it's not an offence to carry out development without planning permission.

So far we've used the word 'development' in a general sense, but in town and country planning the word has a specific meaning: it covers only building work and changes of use of buildings and land, even though, in the latter case, no actual construction need take place. The term 'developer', strictly speaking, means anyone who carries out development but generally refers to companies who undertake development for profit rather than for their own use or occupation. Throughout this book, we use the term 'applicant' rather than 'developer', for any individual or organisation involved in development. The words 'planning permission', 'planning consent' and 'planning approval' all have the same meaning.

FACTORS THAT INFLUENCE PLANNING DECISIONS

Sadly, considerable energy spent in opposing or trying to change development proposals is wasted because objectors focus their efforts on irrelevant points and on factors that aren't taken into account when making planning decisions. Legally, the various planning authorities have to follow the policies of the county Structure Plan and district council's Local Plan, or of the Unitary Development Plan, unless 'material considerations' indicate otherwise.

FIGURE 1.1 Operating the Planning System

Authority	Personnel	Functions
Secretary of State for Local Government, Transport, and the Regions (DTLR), Northern Ireland Assembly, Scottish Executive and Welsh Assembly	members of the government and their departments of civil servants	• draw up national planning policy • oversee the planning system • decide major planning appeals
Planning Inspectorate in England and Wales; Inquiry Reporters Unit in Scotland; and Planning Appeals Commission in Northern Ireland	planning inspectors/ reporters/commissioners	• hold Local Plan inquiries • decide and report on planning appeals
County councils in England	elected councillors and planning officers	• draw up Structure Plans, Minerals Plans and Waste Plans • decide planning applications for minerals and waste • advise district councils
District, borough, city Councils (England) Councils (Scotland) County borough and county councils (Wales) Divisional Offices, Northern Ireland Department of Environment	elected councillors and planning officers	• draw up Local Plans • decide most planning applications • take enforcement action

Structure, Local and Unitary Development Plans

Structure Plans are documents containing broadly-based county council policy for planning development across a county. Policies cover issues such as environment, housing, transport, employment, tourism, minerals and waste, as well as particular land uses such as industry, retail, agriculture and recreation. Structure Plans also contain the county council's objectives, explanations and justifications for the policies.

Within the framework of Structure Plans, there are more detailed Local Plans, which translate national and county-wide development policies to district level (see Chapter 5). For example, the government states how many houses should be built in a county. This figure appears in the county Structure Plan, which also allocates the number between the districts. A Local Plan then has to show where that number of new houses can be built.

Unitary Development Plans (UDPs), drawn up by single-tier local authorities, combine the sort of policies included in both Structure and Local Plans, in a single document.

Material Considerations

'Material considerations', to be taken into account when deciding a planning application, aren't exhaustively defined. They can include government advice, as laid down in Planning Policy Guidance Notes and circulars in England, or Planning Policy Statements in Northern Ireland, or National Planning Policy Guidance and Planning Advice Notes in Scotland, or Technical Advice Notes in Wales (see Figure 1.4). In addition to 'statutory plans' (approved Structure Plans, Local Plans and UDPs), councils sometimes have non-statutory or informal planning guidance documents, which set out the council's views on development issues, such as guidelines for building design (see Figure 1.5). Although informal planning guidance shouldn't be given the same weight as statutory plan policy, it is influential. Informal guidance documents usually contain background information relevant to the topic and give guidelines for development. Councils, perhaps not surprisingly, follow the informal guidance they've drawn up themselves rather more closely than do government planning inspectors.

Some areas and buildings, such as Green Belts and Listed Buildings are legally subject to tighter planning control, which the council must also bear in mind when making a planning decision. In addition to these statutory special designations, some councils apply other designations of their own making such as 'areas of attractive landscape', 'strategic gaps', 'areas of high townscape value' and 'local countryside gaps' between villages. These designations, however, don't have their basis in law and, therefore, don't have the same importance as statutory special designations (see Chapter 6).

Other examples of 'material considerations' that can influence a planning decision are points specific to a particular site, such as its history and layout, architecture and design, services, wildlife habitats, access and traffic, and effects on other people (see Figures 2.4 and 2.8).

Another, much publicised material consideration, is the Human Rights Act, which came into force across the UK in October 2000, and its full impact won't become clear until it's been thoroughly tested in the courts. So far, only a few planning appeal cases have been influenced by human rights issues, and some of those are subject to court challenges. The balance between individuals' rights, as protected by the provisions, and the wider public interest, as protected by planning law, has yet to be established but human rights breaches could be a relevant factor in a planning decision.

FIGURE 1.2 Development Allowed Without a Planning Application

These are some of the most commonly used 'permitted development' rights (England and Wales)

Domestic

Extensions and loft conversions	• up to 15% or 70 cubic metres (2,470 cubic feet); • terraced houses and houses in Conservation Areas, National Parks, Areas of Outstanding Natural Beauty or the Broads up to 10% or 50 cubic metres (1,765 cubic feet); • maximum in any case 115 cubic metres (4,060 cubic feet); • not higher than, or nearer a road than, the existing building, nor extend a roof slope facing a road
Porches	up to 3 square metres (32 square feet) and 3 metres (10 feet) in height
Garages, sheds, swimming pools, tennis courts etc	not closer to a road than the house, or higher than 4 metres (13 feet); the total area covered by outbuildings must not exceed 50% of grounds
Paving, surfacing and drives	no restrictions

Minor works

Walls and fences	up to 2 metres (6 feet) high or 1 metre (3 feet) next to a road
Painting outside of buildings	no restrictions

Irrelevant considerations

It's hard to say absolutely that a particular factor is never relevant to a planning decision, but the following are generally not taken into account:

* personal circumstances of the person applying for planning permission (the applicant) and occupiers
* identity of applicants and occupiers
* private or particular individuals' interests, eg views
* benefits offered by applicants not related to the development

FIGURE 1.2 Development Allowed Without a Planning Application Cont...

Temporary buildings and uses
- Buildings needed on a temporary basis associated with building works
- Temporary uses of open land up to 28 days a year, or 14 days for markets and motor racing

Agricultural
Farms of over 5 hectares (12 acres)

Farm buildings	up to 465 square metres (5,000 square feet), subject to limitations including not within 400 metres (437 yards) of a house if the building is for livestock

Farms of 0.4 - 5 hectares (1 - 12 acres)

	extensions and alterations to farm buildings; installing plant and machinery

Industrial

Extensions or alterations to buildings	up to 1,000 square metres (10,000 square feet) or 25%; in Conservation Areas, National Parks, Areas of Outstanding Natural Beauty or the Broads, 500 square metres (5,000 square feet) or 10%

Other categories of 'permitted development' concern development under these headings:

Caravan sites	Forestry	Private road repairs
Services repairs	Local authorities	Highway authorities
Drainage bodies	Environment Agency	Sewerage undertakers
Statutory undertakers	Aviation	Mining operations
Coal mining	Mining waste	Mineral exploration
Mineral deposits	Telecommunications	English Heritage
Amusement parks	Road information	Toll road facilities
Demolition	Education/hospital buildings	CCTV

- commercial competition (the main exception being out-of-town commercial development, in which the effect on the town centre is considered)
- concern about setting a precedent (unless there are specific similar circumstances where one decision might be followed by others that would be harmful)
- other legislation or regulations, such as gaming laws, liquor licensing, environmental health or building regulations
- financial viability of a scheme

FIGURE 1.3 Changes of Use

Planning permission is not needed for changes between any of the uses within each section

Shops	shop, retail warehouse, post office, ticket or travel agency, sandwich bar, hairdresser, undertakers, showroom, domestic hire shop
Financial and professional services	bank, building society, financial and insurance services, estate agents, employment agency, betting shop
Food & drink	restaurant, wine bar, cafe, pub, takeaway
Business	office, research and development, light industry
Non-residential institutions	clinic, consulting rooms, health centre, creche, nursery, day centre, school, college, training centre, art gallery, museum, library, public hall, exhibition hall, church, church hall
Leisure	cinema, concert hall, casino, bingo hall, disco, dance hall, swimming bath, skating rink, gymnasium, sports hall, laser games

Uses not included in any of these categories, and therefore needing planning permission, include: theatre; amusement arcade; dry cleaners; petrol station; car showroom; car hire; taxi business; scrapyard

Planning applications are not needed for changes between these uses:

From	To
Financial and professional services	Shops
Food and drink	Shops
Food and drink	Financial and professional services
Business	Warehousing, storage and distribution (up to 235 square metres/2,350 square feet)
General industry	Business
General industry	Warehousing, storage and distribution (up to 235 square metres/2,350 square feet)
Warehousing, storage and distribution	Business (up to 235 square metres /2,350 square feet)

Human susceptibilities

Planning decisions usually involve weighing up conflicting factors, and judgements between them can be finely balanced. In these circumstances, human susceptibilities can play a part and this is most evident in council decisions. Planning inspectors, inquiry reporters and commissioners, who decide appeals and report on Local Plans, are professionals obliged to set out reasoning behind their decisions in public documents, which are open to challenge in the courts. Inspectors, reporters and commissioners aren't dependent on the local electorate for their positions.

Councillors, on the other hand, are laymen without professional qualifications in planning. Although planning officers give technical advice, a councillor's grasp of what is a proper planning consideration can be hazy. There are huge grey areas in which even the experts' opinions and understanding differ. Errors can occur innocently but, in many cases, questionable decisions do result from undue weight being attached to factors of dubious relevance to planning.

Where non-planning factors influence a decision, the authority isn't likely to admit it. Decision notices must state reasons for refusing permission; there is, however, no requirement for councils to set out their reasons for granting planning permission.

A few sanctions help keep wayward individuals in check. If a council refuses permission unreasonably, it runs the risk of having to pay the applicant's costs of going to appeal. People affected by poor decisions can challenge them in the courts or make a complaint to the Local Government Ombudsman (see page 56), and, if maladministration is found, compensation can be paid. There is also the criminal law if corruption is involved.

PLANNING APPLICATION DECISIONS

When planning permission is granted, the council always makes the permission subject to conditions, such as the time within which the development must be started. Others may require things like external building materials to be approved by the council. Beyond these, conditions covering a wide range of factors relating to the design and use of a development may be imposed, if deemed necessary, relevant, precise, reasonable and capable of being enforced by the council.

Legal undertakings made by applicants are another means of controlling development, which are wider in scope than planning conditions but used in less than one in a hundred cases. Formally titled 'planning obligations', they are sometimes called 'section 106 agreements' (article 40 in Northern Ireland and section 50 in Scotland) or 'planning agreements' because they are usually agreed between a council and an applicant. Legally binding undertakings can, however, be put forward unilaterally by an applicant without the council's agreement, although not in Scotland. Planning obligations can control the occupation of a development, phasing of construction, or provide for funding of roads, sewers and community facilities. Such benefits, given by an applicant are known as 'planning gain'. At Greenford, London, for example, planning

FIGURE 1.4 Government Planning Policy Documents

ENGLAND
Planning Policy Guidance Notes

PPG1	General Policy and Principles	PPG13	Transport
PPG2	Green Belts	PPG14	Development on Unstable Land
PPG3	Housing	PPG15	Planning and the Historic Environment
PPG4	Industrial and Commercial Development	PPG16	Archaeology and Planning
	and Small Firms	PPG17	Sport and Recreation
PPG5	Simplified Planning Zones	PPG18	Enforcing Planning Control
PPG6	Town Centres and Retail Development	PPG19	Outdoor Advertisement Control
PPG7	The Countryside: Environmental Quality	PPG20	Coastal Planning
	and Economic and Social Development	PPG21	Tourism
PPG8	Telecommunications	PPG22	Renewable Energy
PPG9	Nature Conservation	PPG23	Planning and Pollution Control
PPG10	Planning and Waste Management	PPG24	Planning and Noise
PPG12	Development Plans and Regional		
	Planning Guidance		

NORTHERN IRELAND
Planning Policy Statement

PPS1	General Planning Principles	PPS4	Industrial Development
PPS2	Planning and Nature Conservation	PPS5	Retailing and Town Centres
PPS3	Development Control and Roads	PPS6	Planning, Archaeology and Built Heritage
	Consideration	PPS9	The Enforcement of Planning Control

SCOTLAND
National Planning Policy Guidance

NPPG1	The Planning System	NPPG10	Planning and Waste Management
NPPG2	Business and Industry	NPPG11	Sport, Physical Recreation and Open
NPPG3	Land for Housing		Space
NPPG4	Land for Mineral Working	NPPG12	Skiing Developments
NPPG5	Archaeology and Planning	NPPG13	Coastal Planning
NPPG6	Renewable Energy Developments	NPPG14	Natural Heritage
NPPG7	Planning and Flooding	NPPG15	Rural Development
NPPG8	Town Centres and Retailing	NPPG16	Opencast Coal and Related Minerals
NPPG9	The Provision of Roadside Facilities on	NPPG17	Transport and Planning
	Motorways and other Trunk Roads in	NPPG18	Planning and the Historic Environment
	Scotland		

FIGURE 1.4 Government Planning Policy Documents Cont...

WALES
Planning Guidance

Planning Policy

Technical Advice Notes

TAN1	Joint Housing Land Availability Studies	TAN11	Noise
TAN2	Planning and Affordable Housing	TAN12	Design
TAN3	Simplified Planning Zones	TAN13	Tourism
TAN4	Retailing and Town Centres	TAN14	Coastal Planning
TAN5	Nature Conservation and Planning	TAN15	Development and Flood Risk
TAN6	Agricultural and Rural Development	TAN16	Sport and Recreation
TAN7	Outdoor Advertisement Control	TAN18	Transport
TAN8	Renewable Energy	TAN19	Telecommunications
TAN9	Enforcement of Planning Control	TAN20	The Welsh Language – Unitary
TAN10	Tree Preservation Orders		Development Plans and Planning Control

permission was granted for industry, warehousing, retail, leisure and open space on 28 hectares (70 acres), subject to a planning obligation providing for funding public transport and road improvements, job training, cycle paths and landscaping.

OTHER PERMISSIONS

There are consents other than planning permission which might be needed to carry out development. For example, work affecting a Listed Building requires separate Listed Building consent and demolition in a Conservation Area requires separate Conservation Area consent (see Chapter 6). Such consents are similar to planning permission and applications are usually submitted simultaneously.

Most new building work also needs approval under the Building Regulations to ensure the building will meet health standards and be structurally sound. Building Regulations, which are dealt with by district councils' building control departments, are a technical subject and a completely different regime to the planning system.

Removal of hedgerows requires council permission where the hedge is on or next to agricultural land, paddocks, common land, town/village greens or nature reserves, and are longer than 20 metres. Garden hedges are not covered. A hedgerow removal notice has to be sent to the council, which has six weeks to decide whether the hedgerow is deemed 'important' and whether to prohibit its removal. Unless prohibited within six weeks, removal can go ahead. Councils can impose a fine or order replacement planting, if the regulations are not followed and can take out injunctions to stop hedgerows being removed.

FIGURE 1.5 Design Guidelines for Building Near Houses

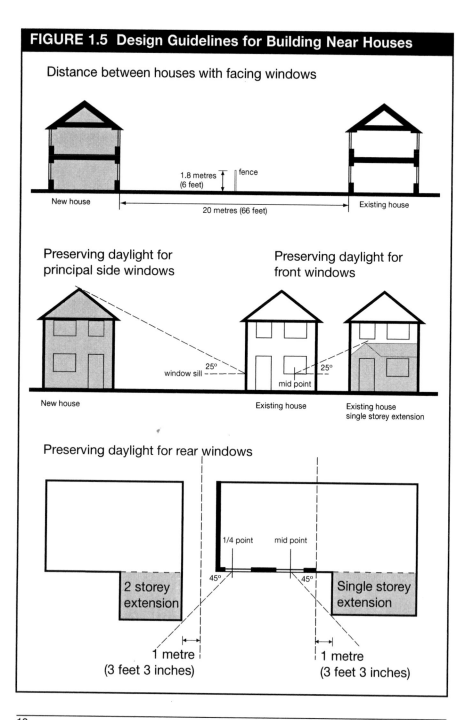

Distance between houses with facing windows

1.8 metres (6 feet) fence

New house

20 metres (66 feet)

Existing house

Preserving daylight for principal side windows

Preserving daylight for front windows

window sill

25°

mid point

25°

New house

Existing house

Existing house single storey extension

Preserving daylight for rear windows

2 storey extension

1/4 point   mid point

45°   45°

Single storey extension

1 metre (3 feet 3 inches)

1 metre (3 feet 3 inches)

Fundamental to the planning system is the need to get planning permission for most new building work and for changes of use of buildings and land. Before development begins, a planning application should be submitted to the council for approval. This is the time to stop and influence the proposed development, if you're worried by it. Armed with the knowledge gained from this chapter, you'll have a good chance of influencing the decision.

Most development occurs after planning permission is granted by district councils, yet the general public is generally unaware development is going to take place until construction is underway. By this time it's too late to object; the time to act is during the course of a planning application (see figure 2.1).

Of the 550,000 planning applications made in the United Kingdom each year, almost 90% receive permission to go ahead with the proposed development. The vast majority of these planning applications are for extensions to small buildings, alterations, loft conversions or building a few houses.

You have the greatest scope for involvement and influence while a planning application is being processed. Once granted, you have no right to appeal against someone else's planning permission (although, in some cases, you can challenge decisions through the courts).

FINDING OUT WHAT IS PLANNED

If you and your community are to make an effective contribution towards planning development in your neighbourhood, you must first monitor the planning applications for development that are being made. These have to be publicised by the council that's going to make the decision by notifying neighbours, displaying site notices or inserting newspaper advertisements. In Scotland, applicants are responsible for advising neighbours. Immediate neighbours are informed by letter of developments that affect only them. Only in Northern Ireland and Scotland, however, is 'neighbour' defined for planning purposes. This Scottish definition of neighbouring land, used for guidance in England and Wales, is:

- any that directly adjoins the application site or is within 4 metres (13 feet) of its boundaries
- where a building is divided, neighbours include properties directly above and below both the application area itself and those parts of the building that come within 4 metres (13 feet) of it
- roads less than 20 metres (65 feet) wide don't count as part of the 4 metres (13 feet)

If development affects a wider area, or there's doubt over adjoining ownership, a notice is put up on the application site so that it's clearly visible from public roads and paths. Large sites, especially where bounded by more than one road, should have more than one notice. Site notices should be left up for at least 21 days. If you see a notice removed or defaced in that period, let the council know straightaway.

Advertisements of planning applications are found in the legal notices section of local newspapers. They're written in semi-legal jargon and appear amongst notices of goods vehicle licences, bankruptcies and council tenders. Lists of all applications appear in some local papers. Newspapers also run stories in their news sections on significant local development proposals.

Parish councils are sent lists of planning applications in their area as, sometimes, are public libraries, Citizens Advice Bureaux, local amenity societies and residents associations. Watch out too for estate agents' boards, especially on undeveloped land. For Sale boards sometimes advertise the fact that the land is being sold for development.

The amount of publicity given to a planning application depends on the nature and scale of the proposed development. For minor development proposals, the council decides whether to notify neighbours or put up a site notice. 'Minor' development means proposals for:

- less than ten houses or a site smaller than 0.5 hectare (1.25 acres)
- less than 1,000 square metres (10,000 square feet) of floor space or less than 1 hectare (2.5 acres)
- developments not involving mining or waste

FIGURE 2.1 Planning Application Procedure

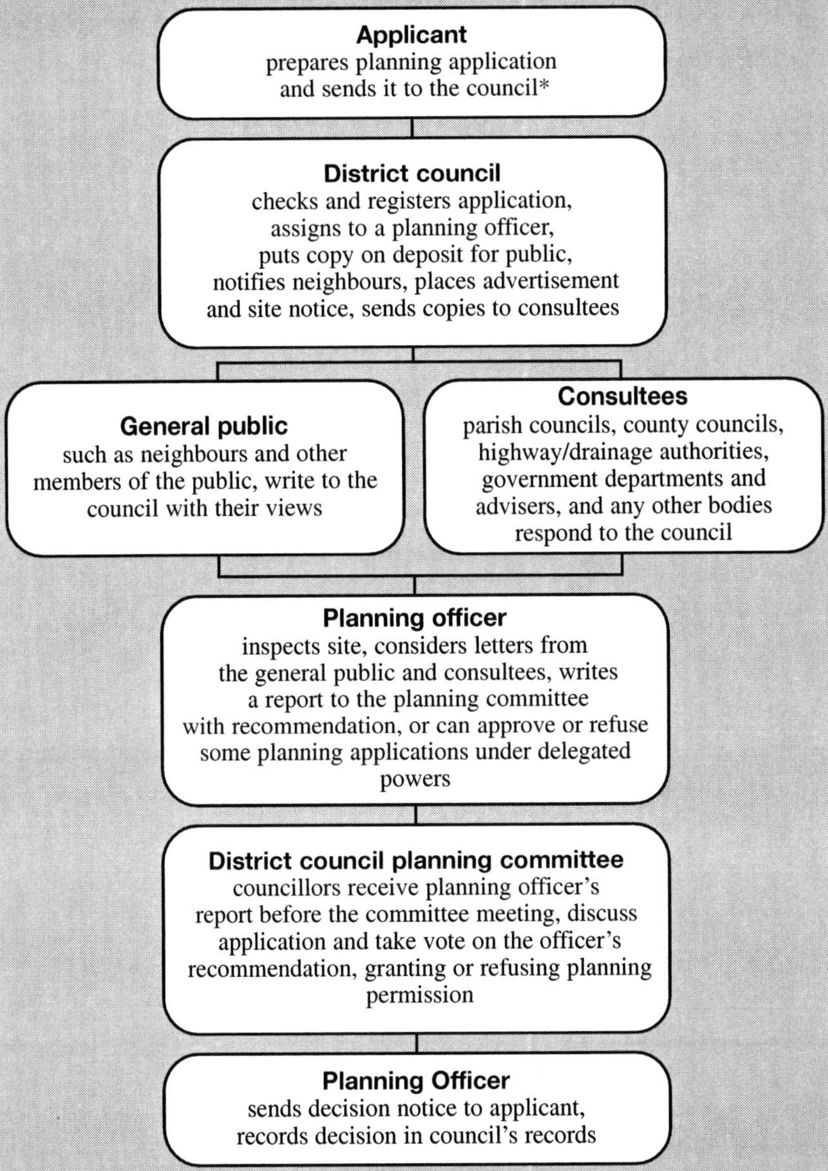

Applicant
prepares planning application
and sends it to the council*

District council
checks and registers application,
assigns to a planning officer,
puts copy on deposit for public,
notifies neighbours, places advertisement
and site notice, sends copies to consultees

General public
such as neighbours and other
members of the public, write to the
council with their views

Consultees
parish councils, county councils,
highway/drainage authorities,
government departments and
advisers, and any other bodies
respond to the council

Planning officer
inspects site, considers letters from
the general public and consultees, writes
a report to the planning committee
with recommendation, or can approve or refuse
some planning applications under delegated
powers

District council planning committee
councillors receive planning officer's
report before the committee meeting, discuss
application and take vote on the officer's
recommendation, granting or refusing planning
permission

Planning Officer
sends decision notice to applicant,
records decision in council's records

* *Planning applications in Northern Ireland are made to the Divisional Planning Office and decided by the Divisional Planning Officer, after consultation with the district council.*

Development above these limits is 'major' development which must be advertised in newspapers in addition to either neighbours being notified or site notices being displayed. Some types of planning application must be advertised in newspapers and have a site notice. These are where:

- an environmental assessment is submitted (see page 33)
- the proposal is not consistent with the Structure Plan and Local Plan
- a public right of way is affected
- a Listed Building or Conservation Area is affected

Because the planning system would grind to a halt if every item of building work and change of use necessitated a planning application, the government makes an order that grants planning permission automatically for specified types of development, called 'permitted development'. There are more than 80 separate classes of 'permitted development'. Before some classes of 'permitted development' can take place, the developer must notify the council. This applies to:

- some agricultural development
- some statutory undertaking development
- some mining and mineral exploration
- some telecommunications and toll road facilities
- demolition

In these cases, the council decides whether it wants to approve details of the proposal, and, if it does, the developer then puts up a site notice.

Councils don't have to publicise some types of planning application although they often choose to. These are:

- reserved matters applications (see page 26)
- changes to applications that have already been submitted
- applications that are submitted only because of a planning condition on a previous planning permission

Beyond these minimum standards, councils often have their own publicity policies, which go farther. Some councils have voluntary site notice schemes: applicants are sent a site notice by the council and asked - but not obliged - to put it up at the property. You can check with individual councils what their policy is. If an application includes land not owned by the applicant, an official notice has to be sent to the owner by the applicant.

SEEING PLANNING APPLICATIONS

Having established that a planning application has been made to the district council, you need to find out the time-scale for action and precisely what is proposed. Relying on hearsay, which might be inaccurate, can render your objection less effective. Planning applications are supposed to be decided in less than eight weeks of submission. This is a target, not a rule, which district councils aim at with widely varying degrees of success.

As soon as you think you might want to object, ask the district council planning department how long you have to submit your comments. This is usually 21 days from when the council notified neighbours or put an advertisement in the paper. Meet this date if you can but all letters received prior to a decision being made on an application should be taken into account by the planning committee. Some categories of application, however, can be approved by the planning officers (see page 37) unless an objection is made. With these applications, the decision may be made at any time after the publicity deadline has past, so it's vital to make your objections promptly.

A copy of every planning application is available for public inspection at the district council's offices during its normal office hours - council planning departments aren't open on Saturdays, only a few open in the evening and some even close for lunch. Copies of planning applications can be purchased from the district council. This can be arranged by telephone, although a payment is normally required before a copy is sent.

You are also allowed to see previous planning applications and various council papers under the Local Government Act 1972. Some cheerfully hand you the whole file; others don't. A few councils charge you to look at certain background papers, which unfortunately they are permitted to do. You can't be charged for seeing applications, decision notices and planning officers' reports to committee.

Planning departments have receptionists or information officers who deal with the public. Although not qualified planning officers, they're often knowledgeable and, in most cases, very helpful. Planning officers are usually on hand to answer queries the receptionist can't deal with although an appointment might be necessary to guarantee meeting a specific officer.

Some parish councils also have copies of planning applications for the public to see. This might be more convenient but they won't be able to answer questions about the proposal.

UNDERSTANDING PLANNING APPLICATIONS

A planning application comprises a completed application form, a certificate of land ownership, plans and drawings including a location plan, and, in some instances, an environmental assessment. It can be submitted with a covering letter or statement explaining or justifying the proposal.

FIGURE 2.2 Application Form

PLANNING APPLICATION

Please read the accompanying notes before answering
each question and write in BLOCK CAPITALS

Date received	22/7/01
Fee paid	£4,320.00
Reference no.	SY/538

1 Applicant
Name and address of applicant
MICHAELS MOTORS
BURTON AVENUE
HAZELDEN
tel no 01581 7777

2 Agent
Name and address of agent
HARRISON ASSOCIATES
ST ANDREWS HOUSE
LIMESTANTON
tel no. 01671 7846

3 Type of application   **Yes/No**

a Full application   YES

b Outline application   NO

c Approval of reserved matters   NO

reference number and date of outline permission ....
which reserved matters are included

siting	design	external appearance	access	landscaping

d Renewal of temporary planning permission   NO

reference no. and date of previous permission ....

e Removal or modification of conditions   NO

reference no. and date of previous permission........................

4 Address of site

Give full address or location. Outline the site
in red on location plan

LAND WEST OF PHOENIX HOUSE
PORTLAND ROAD
SANDLEY

5 Description of development

Give full and accurate description of the
proposed development

ERECTION OF VEHICLE WORKSHOP
AND STORES WITH OPEN DISPLAY
AND STORAGE AREAS AND PRIVATE
CAR PARKING

6 Area of site

Area of application site ...0.5...... ~~metres~~/hectares

FIGURE 2.2 Application Form Cont...

7 Access and parking

Does the proposal include

a new vehicle access ☑

b new pedestrian access ☑

c altering vehicle access ☐

d altering pedestrian access ☐

e provision of parking spaces, ☑

if so how many   34

8 Trees

Does the proposal involve loss of trees or affect any trees; if so, indicate trees on site plan

N/A

9 Existing uses

Describe the existing uses of the property. If vacant, describe the last use of the site

    DISUSED ROWING CLUB

10 Drainage

a How will foul sewage be disposed   PUBLIC SEWER

b How will surface water be disposed   THROUGH INTERCEPTOR TO RIVER

11 Materials

For new building work, state type and colour of all external materials (walls, roof, surfacing, fences). Show materials on application drawings

    COATED PROFILE SHEET STEEL, TARMAC SURFACING
    WALLS DARK GREEN, ROOF OFF WHITE

12 Plans

List all plans and drawings included as part of the application

    LOCATION AND BLOCK PLAN   FLOOR PLANS AND ELEVATIONS

13 Signature
Read and then sign the statement
I apply for planning permission for the development described in this application, and shown on the accompanying application drawings. I enclose a fee of £4,320.00

Signed *M J Harrison*   Date   17th July 2001
On behalf of   MICHAELS MOTORS

Application Forms

Application forms ask all the basic questions about a proposed development (see Figure 2.2). As you go through the form jot down important facts, any questions you have and points of concern that come to mind. Make sure you have at the very least:

- a note of the name and address of the applicant and agent
- the full address of the site
- the description of the proposed development
- the type of application
- the council's application reference number

Forms vary slightly between authorities but these headings are found on most application forms:

Reference number

This is usually written prominently on the form by the council when the application is registered and should be quoted on all matters connected with the application.

Applicant

This is the person making an application or on whose behalf it's made. The applicant doesn't necessarily own any or all of the land, or have the owner's permission to make an application, and can conceal his or her true identity by using another name. Planning permission relates to the application site, not to the person who makes the application. Applications can be made with the intention of selling with planning permission.

Agent

Where an applicant appoints an agent, the council corresponds with him or her, rather than the applicant. An agent is any representative who acts for an applicant or Local Plan objector. Just because an agent is used doesn't necessarily mean that person or firm is qualified or even knowledgeable. Planning consultants are often used as agents, as sometimes are estate agents, solicitors, architects and builders.

Type of application

There are two basic types of planning permission: full and outline. A full application shows all the detail of planning proposals, while an outline application establishes the principle of development, leaving details - the reserved matters (siting, design, external appearance, access and landscaping) - for subsequent submission to the council. Details of the reserved matters should be submitted within three years of the outline planning permission and the completion of an application form isn't compulsory for reserved matters applications. Applications for changes of use, engineering operations and mining can't be made in outline.

The full/outline/reserved matters distinction is important when you frame your objections or comments. For an outline application, you should deal with the general concept or principle of development, such as whether this is the right place for the proposal. Check carefully what details are reserved in the application. Usually all are, but not necessarily. The form should specify this. If the application is for approval of reserved matters, you won't be able to challenge the concept of development. This will have been established earlier when outline planning permission was granted. Your comments in this instance should be directed to the submitted details, which should be consistent with the outline planning permission. On a full application, you can comment on both principle and detail.

Planning applications can be made to vary or remove conditions on earlier planning permissions or to renew temporary planning permission. Ask at the planning department to see the previous application. Look at the decision notice, officer's report to committee and any other information on the file to find out why the condition was imposed in the first place. See if the reasons still apply and whether there's been any change in circumstances. On an application to renew temporary planning permission, you need to look at the existing development to see what problems there have been and whether permission should be allowed to continue.

Address of site

Addresses given can be vague, especially when the proposal is on open land, for example 'land west of London Road, Silsby'. Check that other people who might be concerned about the application will realise where the site is from the address given. It is this address that will be in any newspaper advertisements and lists of applications.

Description of development

This section contains the most important information on the form. The description determines what is applied for and, if approved, what has planning permission. Some descriptions are clear, simple and brief, for example, 'four detached houses'. There would, of course, be garages, drives, fences and garden buildings as well as the houses themselves. If the application is in full, you can check these details on the plans. Other descriptions specify every single element of the proposal; this can obscure the true nature of the application.

Area of site

The figure given should correspond with the area edged with a red line on the location plan. If density of development is an issue, check the calculation of site area yourself.

Access and parking

See whether a new access is proposed, as this can have an impact on appearance, highway safety, traffic generation and pattern of traffic routes. If parking is proposed, compare the number of spaces with the council's standards.

Trees

Application drawings should show which trees on the site would be affected by the development. Check whether any are protected by Tree Preservation Orders (see Chapter 6).

Existing uses

Any activities taking place or that have taken place and any rights to use the site could be crucial to the decision. As planning history/existing uses can be highly relevant to a decision, this sometimes induces applicants to mis-describe or exaggerate the answer to this question on an application form. Your own local knowledge, asking around in the area or looking up the site history at the planning department, might clarify the true situation and provide vital information for your objection.

Drainage

Before planning permission is granted, authorities should ensure the development can be properly drained. The absence of available public or private sewers, unsuitability of land to cope with a private treatment system, insufficient capacity at sewage treatment works and overloading of existing sewers can stop planning permission for development.

Where buildings or hard surfaces are included in an application, rain or surface water has to be disposed of. Constructing a building might mean a different distribution of rain and so reduce the amount of ground over which rain can drain away. This can cause problems in boggy ground, poor draining soil and areas with a high water table. Surface water goes to public surface water drains, soakaways (drainage pits in the ground) or existing water courses (ditches, streams, rivers).

Materials

Full applications should state what external materials are proposed - bricks, tiles, cladding systems - and their colours, as this will affect the appearance and impact of the building. Such details are especially important in Conservation Areas and near Listed Buildings.

Plans

Some forms ask for a list of plans and drawings submitted with an application. With outline planning applications, applicants can submit illustrative drawings, but these should be clearly marked as they don't form part of the formal application. They can nevertheless be important as they show how development might look or prove that it can fit on a site. Revised drawings can be substituted while the council is dealing with an application. The drawings stated on the form might not be the ones on which a decision is finally made. If in any doubt check with a planning officer.

FIGURE 2.3 Typical Drawings to Accompany a Planning Application

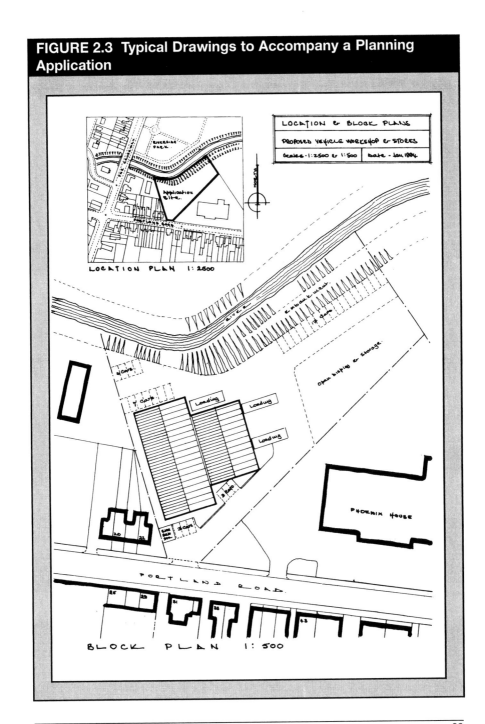

FIGURE 2.3 Typical Drawings to Accompany a Planning Application Cont...

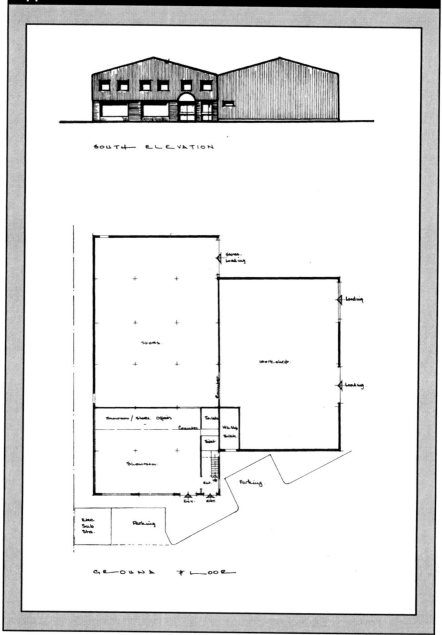

SOUTH ELEVATION

GROUND FLOOR

FIGURE 2.3 Typical Drawings to Accompany a Planning Application Cont...

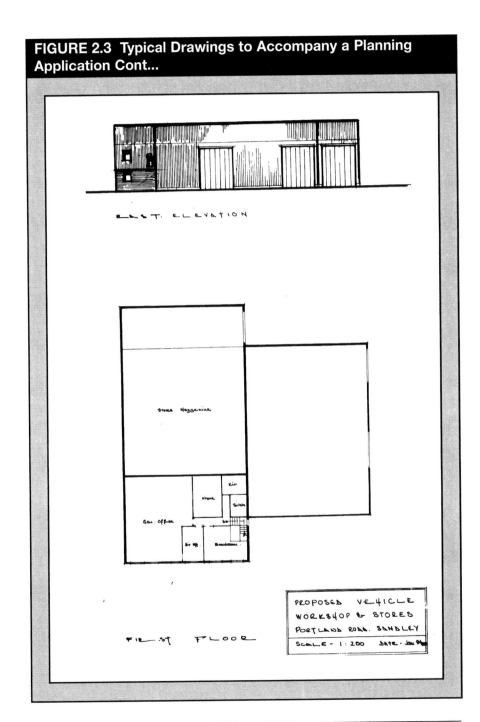

Signature and fees

Forms are signed and dated by applicants or their agents. The eight-week target period for determining applications runs from receipt by the council, not from the date on the form. Delay in submission and registration of applications can occur. Most planning applications require a fee, the level of which depends on the type of planning application, and councils don't usually process applications until that fee is paid.

Other forms

Commercial and industrial development applications must have an additional form, from which much useful information can be gleaned. You can:

- check car parking standards against proposed floor areas
- see what loss of particular uses such as shopping or industry there would be
- gauge activity from staff numbers
- judge the impact of vehicle movements from the numbers given
- find out what processes are involved

There are separate additional forms for agricultural development and mineral extraction.

Certificates of land ownership

Sometimes a certificate of ownership is included in the planning application form, otherwise a separate form is used. Applicants must state whether they own the whole application site, whether anyone else owns the site or part of it, and whether any part is included in an agricultural tenancy. Owners for this purpose include anyone with a lease of seven years or more. Make a note of the owners' names and addresses in case you want to contact them later.

Plans and drawings

Look at the location plan carefully: Ordnance Survey maps, on which most location plans are based, can be well out of date. A location plan sometimes misses off buildings, especially recent development, and neighbours can find their properties or recent extensions aren't shown, for example. Make a note to point out any inaccuracies to the planning officer. A location plan should identify the application site clearly in red and show adjoining properties and roads. All new buildings and areas in which a change of use is sought must be within that line (see Figure 2.3). If the applicant owns or has control over other land nearby, this should be outlined in blue. Blue-edged land is important because the council can impose conditions on planning permission relating to other land the applicant owns. Public rights of way can't be diverted without separate permission, so check the drawings to see what effect a proposed diversion might have. Get a photocopy of the location plan to take away with you, or make a note of site boundaries and adjoining property.

Planning applications for new buildings and alterations will include site or block plans. These should show:

- boundaries, existing and proposed, including subdivision within the site
- existing and proposed buildings
- buildings on adjoining land
- roads, pavements, verges and footpaths
- existing and proposed accesses
- any works proposed to public highways
- parking areas
- trees and other natural features
- proposed landscaping
- existing and proposed drains, sewers, cesspools, septic tanks
- uses to be made of undeveloped parts of the site

In addition to site plans, full applications include floor plans as well as the front, back and side views of buildings. These drawings, which show design and layout, include:

- materials and finishes
- colour and texture of the exterior
- changes in ground level
- construction of access
- position of doors, windows, loading bays

Interpreting drawings and visualising them in three dimensions in the proposed setting isn't always easy, although extensions and alterations are often shaded to help distinguish them. Nor is cross checking separate drawings of the existing and proposed buildings. Check distances to boundaries, distances between buildings, heights of buildings and floor areas with a scale rule. You might need to spend some time studying drawings in order to understand the proposal fully or ask a planning officer to go through the drawings with you. Make notes as you go, jotting down any inconsistencies, inaccuracies, doubts or concerns.

Environmental assessment

Planning applications for a limited number of projects - only a few hundred each year - need an environmental assessment on the effects a proposed development would have on the environment. This is then assessed by the council. Such environmental statements should have a non-technical summary and it is to this that you should refer unless you have a great deal of time or expert knowledge. Make notes and base your comments on this information. Alternatively, if you have funds, get specialist expert help (see Appendix I).

FIGURE 2.4 What to Look for When Inspecting a Site

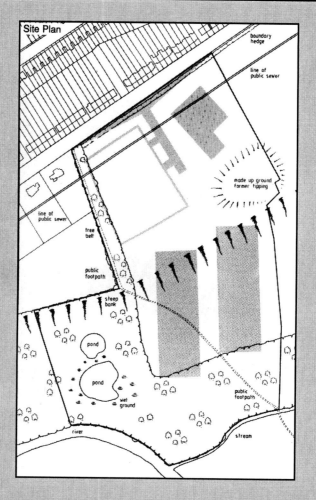

When inspecting the site, you should consider the following points illustrated in this proposal for new buildings, car park and access: effects on houses; loss of boundary hedge to create access and visibility splay; building over public sewer; loss of trees; effect on remaining trees; effect on, and diversion of public footpath; contamination from former tipping; visual impact of construction across change in ground level; effect on wildlife around ponds; pollution of river and stream.

Covering letter/statement

If there appears to be no covering letter or statement with the application, ask a receptionist or planning officer whether a letter was submitted - it can easily have become detached from the forms and plans. Applicants' statements usually contain valuable information mostly, of course, in support of the proposed development. Such information helps you understand an application better and might even allay some of your fears. Beyond this, it can provide you with more ammunition or allow you to refine your arguments. As you go through the letter or statement, note points you disagree with, inconsistencies with the forms and plans, aspects you don't understand and points that you need to check, such as any history and Local Plan policies referred to.

INSPECTING THE SITE

Some points to note when studying a planning application relate to physical factors on and around the site - relationship to nearby properties, safety of access, loss of trees and many others (see Figure 2.4). Unless you're very familiar with the site, go and have a look at it. Take your notes and make a thorough investigation, bearing in mind the points you wrote down.

Even if the site's well known to you, it's still worth walking around the area. View the site from all angles and from all vantage points. Jot down where the proposed development could be seen from, what would be seen next to and near it, and what it would be seen against - trees, buildings or sky. Photographs can be very useful reminders of particular details and features of the site and its setting and they can be included as evidence with your objection.

OBJECTIONS

People concerned about planning applications rarely think to contact the person, agent or organisation making the planning application, but this can produce results. Councils only have power to say 'yes' or 'no' to a proposal or to modify it to some extent by conditions. It's applicants who draw up proposals and they generally prefer these not to be the subject of formal objections in case this sways the planning committee.

You have to gauge for yourself whether it's appropriate to contact a particular applicant. Some are indifferent, not to say hostile, to opposition; yet many are keen not to upset people, especially if they live and work in the community or if they're concerned about public image and bad publicity.

If you decide to speak to the applicant, do it as quickly as possible, so that the application can be revised or you still have time to get an objection to the council. It's particularly worthwhile contacting the applicant if your objection relates to a detail in a proposal, such as the position of a window or the effect on some natural feature. The scheme could perhaps be altered without it being affected overall.

Adopting a friendly rather than a combative approach increases your chances of success. If the applicant is unwilling to talk, concentrate your efforts on the planning

---

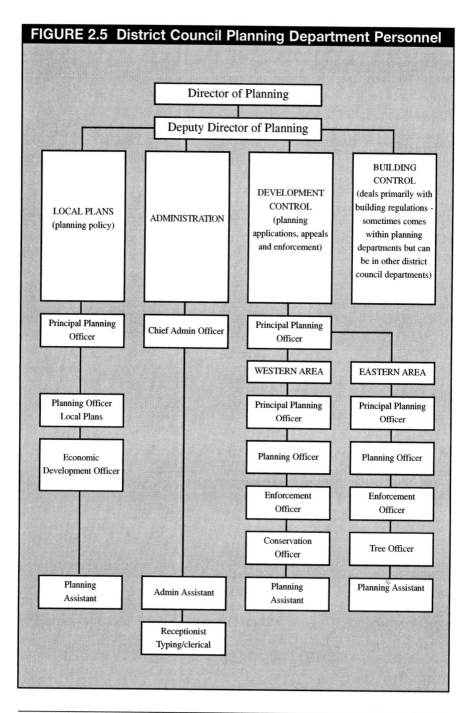

FIGURE 2.5 District Council Planning Department Personnel

Director of Planning

Deputy Director of Planning

LOCAL PLANS
(planning policy)

ADMINISTRATION

DEVELOPMENT
CONTROL
(planning
applications, appeals
and enforcement)

BUILDING
CONTROL
(deals primarily with
building regulations -
sometimes comes
within planning
departments but can
be in other district
council departments)

Principal Planning
Officer

Chief Admin Officer

Principal Planning
Officer

Planning Officer
Local Plans

WESTERN AREA

EASTERN AREA

Principal Planning
Officer

Principal Planning
Officer

Economic
Development Officer

Planning Officer

Planning Officer

Enforcement
Officer

Enforcement
Officer

Conservation
Officer

Tree Officer

Planning
Assistant

Admin Assistant

Planning
Assistant

Planning Assistant

Receptionist
Typing/clerical

officer or councillors instead. If the applicant agrees to make changes, ensure the planning application is formally amended before a decision is made. Do this by checking with the planning department in plenty of time before the planning committee meeting.

Where an applicant doesn't own the application site, you can contact the owner. He or she might know very little about the proposed development and might be concerned that it's attracting opposition or that it might be harmful in some way.

Meeting the planning officer

Large-scale and controversial planning applications are assigned to a planning officer whose role is to assess an application and to write a report on its merits, culminating in a recommendation for approval or refusal of planning permission by the district councillors. Decisions on most planning applications, being minor or uncontroversial, are delegated to planning officers without going to a planning committee. Decisions on planning applications in Northern Ireland are made by the Divisional Planning Officer, not by district councillors.

Find out the name of the planning officer assigned to the planning application in which you're interested and arrange a meeting. If this isn't possible, speak to the officer on the telephone, or better still ask him to come to you. At the meeting have paper and pen handy to record what's said. Referring back to your notes on the planning application, ask the officer to explain points you don't understand. Tell him if you think you found inaccuracies or errors. If you feel an application lacks sufficient detail, discuss this with the officer, as councils can ask applicants to supply additional information and drawings. Explain what worries you have about the proposed development and why. Listen carefully to what the officer says: you could be mistaken about some aspects. It might be that, in this particular case, the council has no choice but to grant planning permission.

Ask the planning officer which plans and informal planning policy documents are relevant to the proposal. He should be able to show you the documents and point out which sections and individual planning policies apply. Write this down for future reference.

Remember when you're talking to the planning officers that they're limited in their realm of activity. They're not concerned with other types of control - vehicle operators' licences, water supply, off-licences, environmental health rules - nor with private legal matters, such as disputes over land ownership, boundaries and covenants. Always be polite and courteous. A sympathetic planning officer can be a very useful ally so try to get a good rapport going and stay in touch with him.

Get the officer's views on what you can do about the application and don't dismiss his advice lightly - yet you should not let yourself be put off if you're not convinced. Even at an early stage the planning officer can often give you a good idea of what the decision or recommendation is likely to be. Remember that, although the recommendation is important, it's the councillors who actually make the decision on contested applications and they're not bound to follow their officers' advice.

FIGURE 2.6 An Effective Letter of Objection

District Planning Officer
Fletton District Council
Remington Street
Thatton
                                                                    17th October 2001

Dear Sir

PLANNING APPLICATION REFERENCE AT/4/01
LAND TO REAR OF CHURCH ROAD, PENFOLD

I wish to register an objection to this application for industrial units. The reasons for my objection are
as follows:

1 Planning Policy

The proposal conflicts with policy H3 of Fletton District Local Plan. This requires that new industrial
development be sited away from existing residential areas. The site is partly in a residential area.

Part of the site protrudes into the countryside, beyond the 'Built -up Area' boundary line shown on the
local plan map. Countryside policy EMP9 specifically states 'applications for new industrial
development will not normally be allowed outside the 'Built-up Area'.

2 Planning History

The site was used as allotments until four years ago and has never been a 'car storage yard' as stated on
the application form. There is no history of industrial use on this site.

3 Site Layout

The proposal represents over-development of the site. The layout is very cramped and would require
the removal of a mature oak tree which contributes to the character of the area. This tree is not shown
on the application plans.

There is inadequate vehicle manoeuvring space on the site. There are only three parking spaces and this
does not comply with your council's parking standards.

4 Effect on Neighbouring Property

The industrial units include first floor offices whose windows would overlook the rear of houses and
back gardens in Church Road, removing our privacy completely.

5 Effect on Surrounding Area

The proposed buildings are of a stark, industrial design, out of character with the brick cottages of
Church Road. The buildings would intrude into open countryside to the rear of Church Road. They
would be prominent, especially from the adjoining public footpath, and visually damaging in the
landscape.

The development would attract commercial traffic on to Church Road, which is a narrow residential
road. The access is near a bend so that increased traffic movements and additional on-street parking
would create safety hazards.

6 Conclusion

This proposal conflicts with Local Plan policies, will create traffic hazards and would be wholly out of
place in this residential road. Privacy at the rear of our houses will be lost. The severity of the
overlooking problem can best be appreciated from my back garden. Please come and look for yourself
when you visit the site.

A number of my neighbours object to this proposal and will be writing to you independently. We
believe this application should be refused as it would be entirely inappropriate and harmful in this
location.

Yours faithfully

Planning departments have a hierarchy of officers (see Figure 2.5). Try to establish the position in the hierarchy of the officer you talk to. Just because an officer appears sympathetic with your concerns - or even agrees with you entirely - that view doesn't necessarily prevail. Planning officers always maintain they are completely independent of elected councillors, yet this isn't always true. The degree of independence varies between authorities. The fact is that planning officers are employed to do the bidding of their employer – the council - not to give out impartial professional advice.

Contacting councillors

Since it's councillors who make up the planning committee and who ultimately decide large-scale and contested planning applications, they're the people who need to be convinced of your case for influencing a proposed development. Sometimes a single councillor speaking forcefully at a committee meeting can turn the tide of opinion. What would otherwise have gone through on the nod can, through a councillor's intervention, be refused or conditions insisted upon. Even if the planning officer recommends refusal, don't presume the planning application will definitely be turned down: an applicant might be working hard on councillors, and so it's up to you to do the same. Most planning applications are not actually discussed at committee meetings, since there are likely to be 20 to 50 applications on any agenda, and so the officer's recommendation is usually accepted. It's the minority that are talked about.

Some 20 to 30 councillors will be on a planning applications committee, and some councils have more than one planning committee. These can be split geographically or just divided into two or more groups to spread the workload. If you have any personal contacts on the council speak to them first and ask around people in the area to find out if they have a friend who is a councillor. Contacts in political parties or local organisations could introduce you to a councillor. Otherwise, get the name, address and telephone number of council members from the district council, together with a note of those who sit on the planning applications committee. Most councils produce year books listing councillors' names, addresses and political affiliations, various committees and dates of committee meetings. It's best to contact councillors who are actually on the planning committee, although if your local councillor isn't, he or she might still take an interest as might the councillor for the area in which the application site is located. In Northern Ireland councillors don't make decisions on planning applications but are consulted, and there's a procedure for resolving cases in which the Divisional Planning Officer and district council don't agree.

Lobbying councillors can sometimes prove counterproductive and needs to be done with care. Some councils discourage lobbying altogether as a matter of policy whilst some individual councillors discourage lobbying on a personal basis. Find out by telephoning the council before you appraoch a councillor. Try to contact them at times likely to be most convenient to them - at their weekly surgeries, if they hold one, or during office hours or early evening. Don't overdo it; harassing councillors won't help your case so avoid getting into an argument if your opinions differ.

FIGURE 2.7 An Ineffective Letter of Objection

17*th* March 2001

Dear Sir

I was so shocked and dismayed to read of the
development plans next door to my house. Surely it is
time to put a stop to this sort of thing before the whole
countryside is swallowed up in one huge industrial
estate. The developer is obviously only in it for the
money. *HE MUST BE STOPPED!*

I have enjoyed my views for *15 years* and these
eyesores will ruin it. Why oh why does this sort of
thing have to go on? I can only guess that someone at
the council is putting something in his *pocket* to let it
through!

Just think of the mud and mess. We have already had
the road up three times and we simply will not put up
with more disruption. If they must build industrial
buildings, surely they can put them up
SOMEWHERE ELSE. I will be speaking to my
MP.

Yours faithfully

Deke McClelland

Make your contact with councillors early and don't be surprised if, especially when an application has only just been submitted, a councillor isn't aware of the proposal. He isn't likely to be familiar with the detail of an application, unless his attention is drawn to it specifically. Tell the councillor what the application is about, give him the reference number, and explain why you're concerned. Be diplomatic; perhaps ask what his views are before explaining what you think is wrong with the proposal. Try asking for his advice on who else to contact and what else to do. If there might be a political angle on the application, let the councillor know. For example, where the controlling group on the council is backing a proposal, the opposition might make political capital by taking up the case against. Planning committees occasionally hold site visits, so if you think it would help your case, ask the councillor to press for a committee site visit. This is also likely to delay a decision on the application and give you extra time to get support for your campaign.

Conclude your conversation by asking what the councillor will do. Usually he'll investigate the application and speak to a planning officer. If you occupy a property next door or near the application site, invite the councillor round to see things first hand. Follow up your initial contact close to the planning committee date to discover the latest information and try to cultivate the councillor's goodwill. This is especially useful if you want to object to a number of different planning applications as it can give you an insight into how the council will react to proposals.

As an alternative to meeting the councillor, ring him up or write. Avoid writing a long letter; stick to one side of a single sheet of A4 paper if at all possible. Councillors are generally busy people and a long detailed letter might not be read at all. Summarise your concern with a few brief points and possibly attach a copy of your letter of objection. Don't be shy about trying to get in touch with councillors. They're elected to serve the community and to represent the local electorate's views. You'll find most councillors diligent and sympathetic, even in cases where they're not able to help you.

Letters of objection

Once you've studied the planning application, been out to the site, spoken to the planning officer and, possibly, contacted the applicant and/or councillors, you should possess the raw material needed to make your objection or comments suitably convincing. An objection in writing is read by the planning officer, noted in the officer's report to committee and put on the application file. That file isn't made publicly available until a few days before a decision is made, when it can be read by members of the public, including the applicant.

Before you write your letter, get clear in your mind precisely what it is you object to. For example, you might be opposed to particular uses wherever and whenever they are proposed - nuclear facilities, gambling or slaughterhouses. Alternatively, a development proposal could be acceptable to you, in general terms, but you believe the site chosen isn't the right place for it - wind turbines in a National Park, scrap metal yard

FIGURE 2.8 Grounds for Objecting

Planning policy
- conflict with Structure Plan, Local Plan or UDP policies
- contrary to government planning policy guidance
- not complying with council's informal policy guidance
- prejudice comprehensive development of an area
- exceptional personal circumstances

Special designations
- loss of important Tree Preservation Order trees
- 'inappropriate development' in Green Belt
- harm to landscape of National Park or Area of Outstanding Natural Beauty/National Scenic Area
- threat to wildlife or geological features of Site of Special Scientific Interest
- conflict with character of Conservation Area
- damage to historic or architectural value of Listed Building
- harmful to the setting of Listed Building
- destroying archaeological remains or monuments

Planning history
- losing important socially beneficial uses
- reducing housing accommodation in area of housing shortage
- other applications refused and no change in circumstances
- contrary to inspector's views in previous appeal decision
- incompatible with existing planning permission

Site considerations
- over development
- insufficient garden or amenity land
- lack of private space
- excessive bulk or scale
- introducing unnatural features
- spoiling natural or existing contours
- incompatible with the design of existing buildings
- loss of important trees, hedges or other vegetation
- threatening a public right of way
- insufficient parking spaces
- failure to meet council's access and on-site turning standards
- loss of important wildlife habitats
- harm to rare plants or animals
- destroying traditional field patterns
- loss of high-quality agricultural land
- public sewers inadequate
- risk of flooding or creation of flood risk
- threat to health of occupants through previous contamination

FIGURE 2.8 Grounds for Objecting Cont...

Neighbours
- overlooking adjoining properties
- blocking natural daylight
- generating noise, disturbance, smells, pollution
- unsociable hours of operation

Surrounding area
- dominating nearby buildings
- conflict with the pattern of development
- poor relationship with adjoining buildings
- visually damaging in the landscape or in the setting
- conflict with the character of the area
- environmental damage caused by vehicles
- inconvenience for pedestrians
- road system is inadequate
- prejudice highway safety
- loss of open spaces
- losing historic street pattern
- adverse effect on rural economy
- adverse effect on economy and businesses
- loss of employment or traditional industries
- threat to viability and vitality of town centre
- creating imbalance between jobs and homes
- failure to meet housing needs
- better alternative sites available

near a residential area, housing on an attractive open space in a town or a road through a Site of Special Scientific Interest. In other cases, you might not be opposed to the development in principle or the chosen site, but you do object to one or more aspects of the particular scheme put forward - poor design, excessive scale, access badly sited, damage to trees, hours of use or problems of overlooking.

The scope of your arguments depends upon the type of application being made (see page 26). Consider whether your objection is to some detailed aspect that could be overcome by the council imposing a condition on a planning permission. Conditions could cover protection of trees, use of certain building materials on the outside of a building, limiting the number of storeys or closing an access. There are limits on what conditions can achieve, however, so raise this with the planning officer.

Bear in mind planning applications occasionally offer opportunities to clean up or improve land and buildings: allowing development on part of a site can mean the remainder is landscaped. The re-use of a derelict building might mean it's repaired, maintained and kept secure so it might be preferable to accept the development while trying to limit its impact and pushing for benefits.

How you write your letter and what you say are a personal matter but here are a few tips to help give your letter of objection maximum impact (see also Figure 2.6). Such tips might appear obvious but you'd be surprised how many people elect not to follow them (see Figure 2.7). When writing your letter of objection,

Do:

- use the notes you made when studying the planning application
- limit your comments to the actual development proposal concerned
- base your arguments on known facts
- back up your assertions with evidence where you can
- concentrate on planning issues (see Chapter 1)
- explain why the proposal would be harmful and to whom
- make your points as brief and concise as you can
- be as specific in your claims as you can
- type the letter if possible, failing that, write very clearly
- quote the application reference number and address of application site

Don't:

- exaggerate the likely effects of the proposal
- make personal remarks about the developer or his motives
- limit your comments to your own personal interests and concerns
- make assumptions as to the applicant's intentions
- include factors unrelated to the use of land, such as the value of your property (although the reasons why your property would be devalued might be relevant)
- make unsubstantiated claims
- use emotive generalisations (eg "we've had enough development")
- underline, USE CAPITAL LETTERS or exclamation marks in the text!!!

A full and comprehensive letter of objection to a planning application should include some or all of the following topics (see Figure 2.8), although there could well be others you can think of and use:

- planning policy
- special designations
- planning history
- site considerations
- neighbours
- surrounding area
- miscellaneous

Planning Policy

The Local Plan is the basis for most decisions (see Chapter 5). Study it at the district council planning department or local library, or buy a copy from the council. Look up relevant issues - housing, employment, traffic, environment and others. Look up any policies the planning officer mentioned or policies the applicant referred to in the planning application. Find the application site on the proposals map, included with the plan. There might be a specific policy relating to the site, or to the area where it's located. If so, see what it has to say. Local plans generally show areas where councils think that various kinds of development are appropriate or inappropriate.

In your letter refer to policies which are relevant and support your contentions. Say in what way the proposed development conflicts with the Local Plan. If you can, add why that would be harmful in this particular case.

Also, ask the planning officer if there are any relevant informal policy documents giving general guidance or a development brief for the site. If there's any relevant informal policy, see how the planning application measures up and point out any conflicts with that policy in your objection letter.

Special designations

Ask the planning officer or see for yourself whether the site is covered by a special designation such as Area of Outstanding Natural Beauty, Green Belt, Conservation Area, or Listed Building (see Chapter 6). In most cases any such areas are shown on the map in the Local Plan. If the proposal affects a Listed Building, check whether a separate Listed Building consent application has been made. In deciding planning applications, the effect the proposed development would have on trees covered by a Tree Preservation Order can be important (see Chapter 6). The loss or threat to protected trees is a valid reason for objecting to development proposals, although such trees aren't sacrosanct and a balance with other factors must be made. The age, species, health of trees, the contribution the tree makes to the appearance of the area, the distance to proposed buildings and compatibility of the development with nearby trees all have a bearing.

In the Local Plan read through the sections on development in specially designated areas. These point out particular features and might help guide your thinking on the effect the development being proposed would have on the area.

Planning history

While you're at the planning department studying the application or Local Plan, ask to look up the planning history of the property. Some councils have computer records or cards for each property which show the date and reference for each application, what decision was made (refusal or approval), the date of the decision, and whether an appeal was made against the decision, together with the outcome (see Figure 4.1).

Potentially, any previous planning decision can provide useful material for objections: for example, planning permission for a similar scheme might have been refused and possibly a subsequent appeal dismissed. This doesn't create a legal precedent, however, and a subsequent scheme won't automatically be turned down. Ask for the file on any rejected application and see why it was refused and if the current proposal overcomes previous objections. Try to establish whether there are any other changes in the circumstances.

Previous planning permissions, even when they've lapsed, can tie a council's hands in making its decision: for example, the suitability of the site for the development could already be established. See what differences there are between these previous planning permissions and what's now put forward. The applicant could be keen on securing a few more units or a bit more floor space. The arrangement or layout could be different. Some new buildings might have been erected since the previous planning permission was granted or a new Local Plan might have come into force with different policies.

In your letter it could also be advantageous to mention the type, nature and level of existing use as these can be relevant to a decision, especially if this differs from that stated by the applicant.

Site considerations

In your objection letter, describe briefly the existing features of the site, such as shape, slope, trees and vegetation, and boundaries, then go on to say how they'd be affected and the harm that would cause both to the specific site and to the area. You can attach photographs to your letter to help make or emphasise a point.

Neighbours

Looking at your notes on the application drawings and notes you took at the site, try to visualise the effect the development will have on neighbours. Think too about likely effects of the use - noise, increased activity, smells, and pollution.

If you're actually a neighbour yourself, resist the temptation to exaggerate or to be emotional. Be objective and specific: if, for example, you're concerned about noise or losing natural daylight, say which properties have windows facing the application site and for what purpose the rooms closest to the development are used.

Surrounding area

Refer to the notes you made on site and describe briefly the setting of the application site, its prominence, its relationship to other buildings and uses, and the road network. Then say what the effect of the development would be. If you feel a proposal would spoil the area, say what's significant about the land or buildings concerned, and what would be affected, and how seriously. The affects could be visual, health, safety, noise, employment, housing conditions and many others. Use photographs to illustrate views from various points and the nature of nearby properties.

FIGURE 2.9 Example Leaflet

SAVE OUR VILLAGES

Dear Villager,

Do you enjoy living in your village?
Do you value the convenience of being able to shop on foot?
Do you like to meet friends in the local shops?
Do you value the personal service they give you?
Do you value the way of life of your village?
Do you want to see your way of life ruined?

The new **TESCO** development could destroy **everything** you care about.

What new **TESCO** development? The **SUPERSTORE** that TESCO are intending to build on Little Hammonds Farm, Burgess Hill.

This **SUPERSTORE** will be **ONE MILE** from Hassocks.

The local press has told you that this development has been rejected – **this is not true**. If you don't object **NOW**, the District Council will let it happen.

According to available figures, this store is nearly **twice the size of ASDA, Hollingbury**. Where are they going to get their customers from?

From all the other traders in the surrounding area, that's where.

An how will this affect YOU?

FACT: Traders directly hit can expect to lose up to **60%** of their business. How **many** do you think will survive?

FACT: Traders not directly affected will lose a considerable proportion of their business from spin-off trade.

FACT: Villages across the country have turned into ghost towns, commuter villages.

WHAT CAN BE DONE ABOUT IT?

On the 11th September there was a council committee meeting. Jack Slaughter and Tony Belcher, two of our local councillors, spoke against this development and gained a guarantee that the idea of a **SUPERSTORE** would be fully investigated.

We also have a number of other local councillors and businessmen on our side.

But **NOTHING** can be done unless **ALL** traders and villagers band together and say **NO** to this development.

WHAT HAVE WE DONE ABOUT IT?

ACTION: We have written to **every** household in Clayton, Hurstpierpoint, Hassocks, Keymer and Ditchling.

ACTION: We have posters in a number of shop windows in your village.

ACTION: Local notice boards are carrying the message.

ACTION: We have designed ready-made letters of objection to the Planning Department for people to sign inside participating shops, together with collection boxes and delivery direct to the Council Offices on a regular basis.

ACTION: We have a list of local, county and national elected representatives to whom we will send all the facts and figures we have collated.

ACTION: Some local organisations (Hassocks Amenities Association etc.) have already pledged support to us.

WHAT CAN YOU DO TO HELP?

The most important action **YOU** can take is to communicate your opinion to the District Council as soon as possible.

Individual letters are preferable as these are looked on more favourably, but if you do not have the time – don't worry, **read on!**

Look out for posters in your local shop windows.

Where you see a poster, you can sign a **pre-printed** letter of objection to the District Council.

You can post your letter in the special **collection boxes** inside participating shops. They will all be delivered to the Council **free of charge**.

Even if you write your own letter, you can still use a collection box and save a letter and stamp.

(Individual letters should be written to: The District Planning Officer, Mid Sussex District Council, Oaklands, Oaklands Road, Haywards Heath, W. Sussex RH16 1SS. Head them 'Burgess Hill Local Plan, Proposed Superstore Development'.)

Lobby your elected representatives. All participating shops will have a reference list of names and addresses, from local to national level. (Take a pen and paper with you!)

This is all you have to do. But whatever you do – **do it quickly!**

WE WILL WIN!

A number of District and Parish Councillors do not want the **SUPERSTORE**. Local traders to not want the **SUPERSTORE**. It's up to you whether you want a **SUPERSTORE** or your village shops and way of life. We feel that the cost is too great. The only way to defeat this development is to make as much noise as soon as possible.

WE NEED YOUR HELP NOW!
Your LOCAL Traders

This excellent example of a leaflet to get support was sent to households by the Action Group for the Preservation of Village Life. It explains the proposal, gives the importance of the issue, tells people how to register their views and states the timescale for action. The campaign persuaded 2,600 people to write to the council - the largest number of letters it had ever received.

Miscellaneous

There might also be technical grounds on which to challenge a planning application: for example, the correct notices haven't been served or the application isn't in the correct form. Unless you're sure of your ground, technical points might best be discussed with the planning officer rather than included in your formal objection.

Finally, if you think the application is inaccurate or there are omissions, suggest the planning officer might care to satisfy him or herself that the plans are accurate or that certain facts are correct or whatever the case might be. Don't condemn the applicant, just raise the points as queries. Occasionally, planning applications are made in languages other than English. If possible, offset any advantage this might give the applicant by getting your letter translated into the same language.

When you're happy with your letter, take a photocopy for your records. Then send the original to the planning department, quoting the planning application reference number.

MOBILISING SUPPORT

In theory, weight of numbers against a proposed development isn't in itself relevant to the planning merits of an application for planning permission. In practice, councils can be swayed by public opinion and pressure. Some applications are turned down partly because - and some only because - of public opposition, councils preferring to turn down an application and let a planning inspector take the decision on appeal.

If you do decide to enlist support, keep your objectives firmly in mind. The three groups of people who can stop development at the planning application stage are applicants, councillors and the Secretary of State (or equivalents in Northern Ireland, Scotland and Wales – see Figure 1.1) and it's these you must influence. Whatever you decide to do, always be responsible in your actions.

Make a list of those affected by the development and who else might oppose it, using your notes on the planning application. Your local library keeps lists of local organisations, such as amenity societies, residents' associations, wildlife and architectural conservation groups, and chambers of trade and commerce, together with contact names and addresses. Residents in Hildenborough, Kent got good support from horse riders in opposing a waste disposal site. The access lane was used by 200 local riders, whose safety would have been threatened by heavy lorries.

Planning a campaign

Your immediate objectives are:

- to alert others to the proposal
- to get across the harm it would cause
- to let them know what they can do about it and when

Start with the people you know - friends, neighbours and others in the area. Check with the planning department who was notified about the application and how. Where a site notice is put up, make certain it stays up and in a readable condition for the full 21 days.

Make up your own notice, preferably on brightly coloured card with large letters. Neighbours and local shops could perhaps be persuaded to display one but you shouldn't put this notice on anyone else's land without consent.

Compile a leaflet and, if resources allow, get it designed and printed (see Figure 2.9). Delivering leaflets can be effective but relate their number and distribution to the type of proposal and the areas it would affect. Almost half those notified by leaflet of a road proposal in West Sussex responded to this form of publicity. To achieve maximum results attach or include as part of your leaflet a form for people to complete or just to sign and send to the council, or possibly to the applicant. Of the 2,700 objections to the Kidderminster, Blakedown and Hagley by-pass, 90 per cent were made on postcards distributed by Friends of the Earth. A leaflet can double as a handbill to give out to people in the street.

Organise a petition. Even though the fact someone objects to a development shouldn't in itself carry much weight, councillors and applicants could still be influenced by popular opposition. A petition of 14,500 signatures was collected as part of a successful campaign to stop a 30 bed hotel and 50 time-share units at Millers Dale in Peak National Park.

Get in touch with local newspapers, which are hungry for good stories - especially where there's controversy. Telephone journalists at the papers and try to get them interested in writing an article on the proposed development. Such stories are the staple diet of many regional and local papers. Supply them with the basic facts about the application - where the site is, who is applying and who is objecting, what's proposed, when it's to be decided and why you object. Local papers like using quotes from local people, so offer to supply these too (with, of course, the consent of the people you quote!).

Contact local radio and television stations if the proposed development is of wider interest than just the immediate vicinity. Again, give them all the relevant information. Tell them about the effect of the development on the area and the level of opposition. If you're very lucky and can involve a national or local celebrity in your campaign, this virtually guarantees media coverage. The involvement of writer John le Carre in opposing a cliff-top farmhouse near his home in Cornwall, secured an article in *The Daily Telegraph*.

If the scale of the scheme is sufficiently large, national newspapers could cover the story - as they did during the protracted public inquiry into the proposed fifth terminal at Heathrow airport. Write to the editor of the paper for the letters page, keeping your letter brief: most letters published are less than 300 words. Anything longer is liable to get edited and it's better you ensure the salient points are included in a short letter.

Arrange a public meeting and invite the press. Meetings in themselves attract publicity and interest and can generate enthusiasm for a wider campaign. The parish council or a local group might provide a hall or even help organise the meeting. Invite speakers such as councillors, planning officers, a planning professional where you employ one, and, if appropriate, the applicant or his or her agent. At the meeting agree tactics, co-ordinate the campaign, delegate action and organise fund raising. Ask whether other objectors are willing to contribute money to a campaign. Use funds for getting professional help (see Appendix I) or printing leaflets, posters, T shirts and badges. Appoint spokesmen or co-ordinators who can meet applicants, councillors and planning officers on behalf of all objectors with greater authority. You have more clout with a body of people behind you.

In all your efforts to inspire others to action, tell them specifically what they need to do and when. Make sure they know when the decision is to be taken. Urge other objectors at least to write to the council.

National campaigning organisations

National campaigning organisations, pressure groups and other bodies might take up your cause, depending on the issues involved. Some, such as the Council for the Protection of Rural England, Open Spaces Society and Friends of the Earth, concern themselves with development generally. The Open Spaces Society co-ordinated objections against proposals by Eton College for a 2.4 kilometre (1.5 mile) long rowing trench in the Thames Valley. Others, such as the Royal Society for the Protection of Birds, Victorian Society, Ramblers Association and Campaign for Real Ale (CAMRA) are concerned with development affecting their specific interests. The Victorian Society and CAMRA, for example, objected to an office block that would have meant demolition of the 200 year old Tommy Ducks pub in Manchester. (See Appendix II for names and addresses of some campaigning organisations).

Make contact with any relevant group as early as possible, giving it all the details you have about the application and urging it to become involved. It might even know about the planning application already through its routine monitoring of development. National campaigners often have representatives experienced in opposing development proposals, so stay in touch with them and co-ordinate your efforts. Don't sit back and leave opposition to another group as they could change their minds or not make all the points you want to put forward. Regard their involvement as a useful addition to your own action.

Becoming a decision maker

You, or your group, could be concerned about development generally in your area and the sort of decisions your council is making. If so, think about getting direct power by standing for election to the district council; rather than relying on others, you'll then be making the decisions yourself. Objectors in Walton on Thames, Surrey formed the Residents Party when Elmbridge Borough Council sold the town hall and open space for redevelopment. They won 19 council seats against Conservatives 23, Liberals 10 and Labour eight and this put them in a powerful position to decide planning applications.

Ownership of property gives ultimate control over its development, regardless of whether planning permission has been granted. If you can raise the money to purchase the land or buildings you can decide what happens to it. The 473 residents of Burton Leonard in Yorkshire raised £175,000 to buy a nursing home to prevent it becoming a rehabilitation centre for drug addicts. Outright ownership isn't even necessary in some situations as contractural arrangements, such as leases or covenants, might be sufficient to preserve or modify uses or prevent certain building work.

Contacting consultees

When a planning application is submitted, the district council consults various organisations that have responsibilities, or knowledge relevant to, or are affected by the proposed development. Consultees include:

- other district council departments, such as environmental health and leisure
- county councils, parish councils
- highway authorities, drainage authorities, waste regulation authorities

FIGURE 2.10 Typical Planning Officer's Report to Committee on an Application

Address   Land adjoining 52 East Drive, Bucklegate

Proposal   Outline, Erection of five luxury cottage-style detached houses

Application No   AN/01/0245

Applicant   AB Builders Ltd

Consultations   *Adj properties:* six letters received, all object, over development, loss of trees, dangerous access.
Petitions: one, attached.
Bucklegate Conservation Group: object, over development out of keeping with attractive low density residential area. Protected trees at risk. Two houses would be acceptable.
Borough Engineer: removal of frontage hedge required to give adequate northerly visibility.

Policies   Borough Plan policies: H2, H3, and ENV7
Structure Plan: no conflict
Conservation Area: not applicable

Site description The application site extends to 0.2 hectares of level grassland. It is bounded by established hedgerows on the east and west boundaries and close board fence on the north and south. There is a group of three protected oak trees in the south east corner.

Site history   Previous application for three pairs of semi detached houses refused, 1987

Comment   Housing development is acceptable in principle on this site. However the cramped form of development proposed is out of character in this low density area. The development, if permitted, would have an incongruous and uncomfortable relationship to the existing pattern of development, contrary to Local Plan policy H2. Although only in outline, concern is expressed over the likely proximity of the rear houses to the protected trees. If permitted, the location of the dwellings could give rise to an application to fell the trees that would be difficult to resist. Due to the size of the access required to serve the development, the frontage hedge must be lost to meet the visibility standards of the Borough Engineer. This proposal has met with unanimous objection from local people and is considered unacceptable.

Recommendation Refusal

Reasons   1. Over development, contrary to Local Plan policy H2
2. Adverse effect on landscape, policy ENV7
3. Unneighbourly, poor relationship to existing development

- English Nature, Scottish Natural Heritage, Countryside Council for Wales, Environment and Heritage Service of Northern Ireland DoE
- English Heritage, Historic Scotland, CADW (Welsh Historic Monuments Executive Agency)
- government departments, such as the Department of the Environment, Food and Rural Affairs
- Environment Agency, Health and Safety Executive
- Sports Council, Theatres Trust
- local police
- railway operators, Coal Authority, British Waterways Board

Ask the planning officer who has been consulted and, if appropriate, find out what comments consultees make. Responses to consultation start coming back to the district council about a month after the application was submitted to the council. In most cases it's not appropriate or necessary for you to contact consultees direct. However, if you're particularly concerned about an aspect of a proposal, get in touch with the relevant consultee. You might just be able to alert a consultee to something, perhaps a local factor, which could affect the response back to the district council. Where consultees are particularly alarmed by a proposal, they can become active objectors themselves. Ask the consultee for information relevant to the proposed development or where you can find sources of more detail. Note what the consultee says and add this to your letter of objection to the district council, refining your arguments and making them more precise.

A parish council's opinion on a planning application can be significant, not least because many parish councillors are also district councillors and parish council recommendations are often followed closely by the district council. In any event, they have personal contacts on the district council and could influence them, so contact local parish councillors. Approach them in the same way as you would district councillors (see page 39). Discuss the planning application and let them know your views.

Lobbying Members of Parliament
The local Member of Parliament doesn't have a direct role in planning decisions and yet in some cases, through political connections, he might have influence with district councillors. Letters from Members of Parliament carry no more weight than letters from members of the public.

Lobbying government
The government has the power to take the decision out of a district council's hands by calling-in applications that would affect wide areas, be controversial nationally or in the region, conflict with national planning policy and where national security or foreign governments are involved. This power is exercised in England by the Secretary of State for Transport, Local Government and the Regions, in Scotland by the Scottish

FIGURE 2.11 Typical Decision Notice Granting Planning Permission

ROSELAND
DISTRICT COUNCIL

Application No. FG/02/875

TOWN & COUNTRY PLANNING ACT 1990

Applicant: Mr D Metcalfe, Barley Street, Upton
Agent: Philips & Partners, Western Road, Boxbridge
Description: Conversion and extension of buildings to six craft workshop units
Address: 24 Commercial Way, Upton

In pursuance of its powers under the above Act, the council hereby GRANT planning permission for the above development, in accordance with your application received on 1/2/02 and the plans and particulars accompanying it.

Permission will be subject to the following THREE CONDITIONS:

1   The development hereby permitted shall be begun before the expiration of five years from the date of this permission.
Reason: To comply with the requirements of section 91 of the Town & Country Planning Act 1990.

2   Prior to the commencement of the development hereby permitted, a schedule and samples of materials and finishes to be used for the external walls and roofs shall be submitted to, and approved in writing by, the local planning authority.
Reason: To secure a satisfactory external appearance in the interests of amenity.

3   Access shall be to Commercial Way only. The existing access to Cromwell Lane shall be stopped up, prior to commencement of the works.
Reason: In the interests of highway safety.

Dated: 1 April 2002

Signed:

Donald Hawksworth-Abbotte
DIRECTOR OF PLANNING
For and on behalf of the council

Executive, and in Wales by the National Assembly. As planning applications in Northern Ireland are decided by the Planning Service of the Department of the Environment, there is no call-in provision, although with major planning applications the Planning Service can decide whether to hold a public inquiry. Examples of called-in applications include:

- Center Parcs UK Ltd - holiday village in the AONB at Longleat estate, Wiltshire
- consortium of English Estates, Allerdale District Council and Cumbria District Council - executive houses in an SSSI at Mary Port, Cumbria
- Scottish Nuclear - dry spent fuel store at Torness, East Lothian

The call-in powers are used rarely - about 150 cases a year throughout the UK. If you're concerned with a proposal of the sort listed above, you can write to the appropriate DTLR regional office, Scottish Executive, or National Assembly for Wales urging the use of the call-in procedure. Controversiality is one of the criteria for calling-in a decision so the more people who write, the more chance there is of the application being called-in. However, you'll need to weigh up whether the government is more likely to refuse the application than the district council. This can happen in cases where the council itself is making or promoting a planning application. Of all applications called-in about a third are given planning permission.

THE DECISION

You can see the planning officer's report on a planning application (see Figure 2.10) a few days before the relevant meeting and get a photocopy. Ask at the planning department the date, time and place of the committee meeting which will be open to the public. Double check that applications that you're concerned with are on the agenda.

If you've spoken to councillors who have promised support, let them know you're going to attend the committee meeting to hear the discussion. They might then speak more forcefully on your behalf, because at many committee meetings neither applicants nor objectors are allowed to speak. You can only sit in the public seating and listen. Have paper and pen handy in case anything said is worth noting for future reference.

About half of all councils now allow members of the public to speak at committee meetings. In Scotland, objectors to applications which are contrary to council's plans have the right to speak. Find out well in advance whether your council has such a policy. Ask for the council's information leaflet on public speaking at committees which will set out what the procedure is and how long you can have to speak. Think whether you actually need to speak. If your other action has been effective it might not be essential but a persuasive or heart-felt speech can give added impact.

Since the planning officer's recommendation is accepted without discussion on most applications, the one you have gone to hear might or might not be discussed and will be decided with or without a recorded vote. Where the committee is divided a formal vote is taken after a discussion about the application.

If you can't attend the committee meeting, you can find out the result of an application at a committee meeting by telephoning the planning department the day after. In England and Wales, councils don't have to notify objectors of decisions, although some do. In Northern Ireland, the Divisional Planning Office notifies objectors of its decisions. In Scotland, councils send decision notices to all objectors. Where planning permission is given contrary to planning policy, Scottish councils should also send out reasons for granting permission.

Four decisions are possible - permission, refusal, delegated or deferred – and there are implications with each.

Planning permission

Planning permission gives the right for a development to go ahead. Look at the decision notice, which is usually available within a week or so of the committee meeting, to see whether permission is subject to conditions and what they are (see Figure 2.11). Discuss conditions with a planning officer if you're in any doubt about their effect. In some cases there'll be a 'planning obligation' controlling the development or requiring the applicant to do something (see Chaper 1). Except for development contrary to development policies in Scotland, councils don't have to give reasons for giving planning permission. There's currently no right for objectors or anyone but an applicant to appeal against planning permission.

Delegated decisions

Decisions are sometimes made in principle but, for technical reasons, not formally made. This happens where:

- a consultation period has not expired
- further information unlikely to affect the decision is awaited
- the council wants revised drawings showing amendments to the scheme
- a 'planning obligation' is to be signed by the applicant before planning permission is given (see Chapter 1)

The formal decision is delegated to the most senior planning officer to make when the outstanding matter is resolved. Contact a planning officer a couple of days after the committee meeting to discover what's happening with a delegated decision. There might be an opportunity for further lobbying or action before a final decision is made.

Deferred decisions

Decisions are deferred in similar circumstances to delegated ones, but where the committee wants to make the decision itself. Applications are often deferred where committee members decide to make a site inspection. This normally means they're uncertain whether planning permission will be approved or refused, so more lobbying might prove useful, as with delegated decisions.

Refusal of planning permission

Refusal of planning permission might be what you seek but isn't necessarily the last you'll hear of the proposed development. Check carefully the reasons given for refusal on the decision notice (see Figure 2.12). If these are for some detail or technical deficiency, the applicant might amend the design, find a new access point or scale a scheme down. If an applicant appeals, the reasons for refusal usually define the main issues disputed at appeal. There's nothing to prevent a revised planning application being submitted a day, a month or a year after refusal.

CHALLENGING PLANNING DECISIONS

Although there's no right for objectors to appeal against planning permission, any council decision can be challenged in the courts on grounds that it wasn't made properly. This is a highly legalistic business requiring the advice of planning lawyers and for this reason an expensive one. If there's a lot at stake and you've got the funds, consult a planning solicitor (see Appendix I).

COMPLAINTS

You can complain to the Local Government Ombudsman if you feel the council handled a planning application badly, treated you unfairly or failed to follow procedure properly. The Ombudsman, however, won't look into the merits of a planning application and can't alter the decision. Complaints are referred to the Ombudsman by the council, or if the council refuses you can make the complaint direct (addresses in Appendix II). Booklets are available on how to go about making a complaint. Planning related cases account for about a fifth of complaints and maladministration is found in a few per cent of the total number of complaints made. Very few cases are pursued beyond the preliminary stage.

PLANNING APPLICATIONS - ACTION CHECK LIST

1   Check with the district council whether a planning application has been made.
2   Ask when comments are supposed to be submitted and when the application will go to a committee for a decision.
3   Study the application, visit the site and make notes.
4   Meet the planning officer to discuss the application and continue to monitor progress.
5   Contact councillors.
6   Write your letter of objection and send it to the council.
7   Alert other potential objectors and the media.
8   See the planning officer's report to the planning committee.
9   Attend the council's planning committee meeting to hear the application discussed, or telephone for the result.
10 Look at the council's decision notice.

FIGURE 2.12 Typical Decision Notice Refusing Planning Permission

HARDING BOROUGH COUNCIL

REFUSAL OF PERMISSION

TOWN AND COUNTRY PLANNING ACTS

Application No.	KG/02/1253
Applicant:	BOWRING CONSTRUCTION
Situation:	SITE AT BARN LANE, KIRKWOOD
DESCRIPTION:	CHANGE OF USE TO STORAGE OF BUILDER'S MATERIALS

In pursuance of its powers under the Town and Country Planning Acts, and all other powers, the Council hereby refuses to permit the development specified in the plans and application specified above, for the following reasons:

1. The development would represent an undesirable commercial use of the land detrimental to the amenities and outlook of nearby residents, contrary to policy RE515.

2. The form and use of the development proposed would be out of character with surrounding properties and visually damaging in the street scene.

3. The proposed development would result in an unacceptable loss of preserved trees to the detriment of the character and amenity of the area, and would be contrary to policy ENV23.

4. The position of the proposed access does not accord with highway safety standards. Impaired visibility at the new junction would present a hazard as would additional traffic movements from stopping turning and manoeuvring vehicles. Consequently, the proposal would conflict with policy TR17.

Dated: 25th March 2002

To: Marshal & Co

   Marine Parade

   Kirkwood

Signed:

S Hageoe

BOROUGH PLANNING OFFICER

Where planning permission is refused by a district council, only the person who made the planning application can appeal for the decision to be reconsidered. An applicant can also appeal if a district council doesn't decide a planning application within eight weeks of receipt. Appeals are made in England to the Planning Inspectorate, in Northern Ireland to the Planning Appeals Commission, in Scotland to the Scottish Executive Inquiry Reporters Unit, and in Wales to the Planning Inspectorate. For convenience, we refer mainly to "Planning Inspectorate" and "inspectors" to include all these bodies and their members. Each year there are around 16,000 appeals in Britain. About one third result in planning permission being granted.

Appeals are dealt with in one of three ways:

- written representations, in which appellants (applicants who appeal) and councils put in statements of their cases
- hearings, in which appellants and councils discuss issues in an appeal in front of a planning inspector, commissioner or reporter
- public inquiries or formal hearing, which are like court hearings but less formal, with an inspector, commissioner or reporter as the judge

About 74% of appeals are decided by written representations, hearings account for around 20% and public inquiries for about 6% of appeals. In Scotland, hearings are uncommon. Planning appeals take decisions on development proposals out of the local scene. There's less scope for lobbying, and public opinion is less influential in appeals. Your action here needs to be fought squarely on planning issues. You shouldn't, however, feel daunted by the semi-legal appearance of the appeals process. The public has a role and, if you want to make your views count, don't hesitate to get involved.

FINDING OUT ABOUT PLANNING APPEALS

About one in five refusals is appealed but it's difficult to predict which applications these will be. Applicants might make it clear at the application stage that they're prepared to appeal. The larger the scheme and the more money that was put into the application, the greater the likelihood of an appeal. Applicants weigh up the reasons for refusal given by councils and decide whether an appeal stands a chance of success. The cost of fighting appeals can put off applicants.

Appeals aren't publicised as widely as planning applications. If you commented on the original planning application, you should be notified when an appeal is made. Your objection letter to a planning application is sent to the inspector and will be taken into account automatically. Organisations that were consulted on the original planning application are also notified. You should be notified separately of the time and place of a public inquiry, if there is to be one. When public inquiries are held, the person appealing puts up a site notice giving the time and place. District councils keep records of appeals submitted. Local papers often run stories about significant appeals but don't rely on this. Ask the planning officer who dealt with the application to make sure you're contacted if an appeal comes in. The safest way to find out if an appeal has been submitted is to double-check periodically with the district council. If you're concerned with one particular planning application, a monthly telephone call to the district council should suffice as appeals have to be made within six months of the original planning refusal. Public comment on planning appeals is subject to strict deadlines so the instant you hear about an appeal, find out by what date your representations have to be made.

An outstanding appeal doesn't stop a new planning application being made so watch out for this. Applicants sometimes appeal to put pressure on councils while trying to negotiate another planning permission.

STUDYING THE APPEAL

Go to the planning department and ask to see the file and the notice of appeal forms, quoting the planning application reference number. If you didn't see the council's decision notice or the planning officer's report on the original planning application, start with them and look at the reasons given for refusal on the notice. These are the basis on which the appeal is fought. See what the officers said about the proposal in their report. Buy photocopies or take notes.

Then study the notice of appeal itself. The appeal form is well laid out and straight forward, being divided into a number of sections (see Figure 3.1). Appeal forms in Northern Ireland, Scotland and Wales vary from the English version but the information required is the same, except the form in Northern Ireland doesn't ask for grounds of appeal.

Check the name of the appellant (an applicant who appeals) is the same as on the original planning application as only applicants can appeal. Note which method of appeal - written representations, hearing or public inquiry - the appellant has opted for. Where appellants ask for written representations, the council can insist on an inquiry. Councils can't insist on written representations where appellants want an inquiry. In most cases, councils go along with written representations.

Ask the planning officer whether the council is to insist on a public inquiry. If it isn't, and you feel a public inquiry would give you a better chance to get your views across, speak to councillors very quickly. Overall, around a third of appeals result in planning permission being given, yet for appeals decided by hearings and inquiries the figure is higher, at around 40%. The council states whether it agrees to the written representations procedure in the appeal questionnaire, which should be completed within fourteen days.

On the appeal form, check that you've seen the documents and plans referred to and make a note of the grounds of appeal so that you can deal with the points in your letter or statement. Then read the council's appeal questionnaire, noting whether there are any special designations, such as Conservation Area or Green Belt and which planning policy documents and specific policies the council says are relevant. Write down the appeal reference number if you don't have it already.

An appeal statement might accompany the other appeal documents but doesn't usually. You should write straight away because, for your comments to be taken into account, you must meet the relevant deadline (six weeks from the start date in England – see Figure 3.2). With written appeals, unless the appellant's statement is submitted early you won't be able to see and comment on it. With hearings and inquiries you can comment on the appellant's statement if you attend the hearing or inquiry.

If you can get hold of a copy of the appeal statement in time to comment, read the appellant's case carefully and make notes. There's no set form for appeal statements, clarity and quality vary widely depending on who writes it. Check factual points; note anything you disagree with. Look closely at any new plans or drawings since limited scope is allowed to revise proposals between planning applications and appeals. If the original application was outline, completely new or different drawings can be submitted so consider the effect of revisions. See what's said about the council's reasons for refusal and if you objected to the original application, see whether these points are addressed. Speak to a planning officer about any aspects you don't understand. Then study the council's statement on the appeal to give you ideas and guide your thinking. Don't miss your opportunity to comment by waiting to see the statements.

FIGURE 3.1 Appeal Form

The Planning Inspectorate

PLANNING APPEAL FORM

For official use only
Date received

Please send each appeal on a separate form

Your appeal and essential supporting documents must reach the Inspectorate within 6 months of the date shown on the Local Planning Authority's decision notice (or, for 'failure' appeals, within 6 months of the date by which they should have decided the application).

Before completing this form, please read our booklet 'Making your planning appeal' which was sent to you with this form.

WARNING: If any of the 'Essential supporting documents' listed in Section J are not received by us within the 6 month period, the appeal will not be accepted.

A. APPELLANT DETAILS

The name of the person(s) making the appeal must be the same as on the planning application form.

Name ___RESIDENTIAL RENTALS LIMITED___

Address ___45 COAST ROAD___   Your reference _____

___SEASIDE___   Daytime phone no ___01717 793252___

_____   Fax no _____

Postcode ___SE37 2FR___   E-mail address _____

B. AGENT DETAILS (if any)

Name _____

Address _____   Your reference _____

_____   Daytime phone no _____

_____   Fax no _____

Postcode _____   E-mail address _____

C. LOCAL PLANNING AUTHORITY (LPA) DETAILS

Name of the LPA ___SEASIDE BOROUGH COUNCIL___   LPA's application reference no ___SE/01/1150___

Date of the planning application ___30/01/01___   Date of LPA's decision notice (if issued) ___09/03/01___

D. APPEAL SITE ADDRESS

Address ___26-30 GEORGIAN SQUARE___

___SEASIDE___

_____ Postcode ___SE37 3SJ___

National grid reference ___HS 846 111___

(Please see the key on an Ordnance Survey map for instructions; this should be 2 letters and 6 numbers. eg TQ 298407)

PINS PF01 (REVISED JULY 2000)   1   *Please turn over*

FIGURE 3.1 Appeal Form Cont...

E. DESCRIPTION OF THE DEVELOPMENT

(This must be the same as on the application sent to the LPA, unless minor amendments were agreed)

CONVERSION TO 20 SELF-CONTAINED FLATS

Size of the whole appeal site *(in hectares)*
0.10 HECTARES

Area of floor space of proposed development *(in square metres)*
400 SQUARE METRES

F. REASON FOR THE APPEAL

This appeal is against the decision of the LPA to:

*Please tick **one** box only* ✔

1. Refuse planning permission for the development described in Section E. ☑

2. Grant planning permission for the development subject to conditions which you do not like. ☐

3. Refuse approval of details listed under a previous outline planning permission. ☐

4. Grant approval of details listed under a previous outline planning permission subject to conditions which you do not like. ☐

5. Refuse to approve any matter required by a condition on a previous planning permission (other than those in 3 or 4 above). ☐

   or The failure of the LPA to give notice of its decision within the appropriate period (usually 8 weeks) of an application for permission or approval. ☐

G. GROUNDS OF APPEAL

If you want your appeal dealt with by the written procedure, your **FULL STATEMENT MUST** be made, otherwise we will return the appeal form. You should give a clear explanation of why you disagree with each of the LPA's reasons for not granting permission, if appropriate. Please continue on a separate sheet(s) if you need to and attach them to this form. If you have requested a hearing or an inquiry, please provide a brief outline of your case.

1   THE HOUSES ARE PHYSICALLY SUITABLE FOR CONVERSION WITH INTERNAL ALTERATION. EXTERNAL ALTERATIONS, INCLUDING NEW DORMER WINDOWS AND EXTERNAL STAIRCASE, WILL NOT ADVERSELY AFFECT THE APPEARANCE OF THE BUILDING. OTHER PROPERTIES IN THE TOWN HAVE BEEN CONVERTED.

2   TARMAC SURFACING OF THE FRONT GARDENS WILL PROVIDE SOME PARKING SPACES. THERE IS IN ANY EVENT ADEQUATE ON-STREET CAR PARKING AVAILABLE IN THE EVENINGS. MOST FLATS IN THE TOWN CENTRE DO NOT HAVE THEIR OWN CAR PARKING SPACES.

2

FIGURE 3.1 Appeal Form Cont...

G. GROUNDS OF APPEAL (continued)

3   THE SCHEME WOULD NOT RESULT IN NEIGHBOURING PROPERTIES BEING OVERLOOKED TO AN UNACCEPTABLE DEGREE. THE FLATS WOULD NOT GIVE RISE TO ADDITIONAL NOISE AND ACTIVITY.

4   POLICY R17 OF THE BOROUGH LOCAL PLAN SAYS THAT IN APPROPRIATE CASES FLAT CONVERSIONS WILL BE ALLOWED IN THE CENTRAL AREA. THE PROPERTY IS CLOSE TO ALL THE TOWN CENTRE FACILITIES. THERE IS A SHORTAGE OF HOUSING IN THE AREA, PARTICULARLY OF SMALL UNITS.

H. CHOICE OF PROCEDURE

Appeals dealt with by written representations are usually decided more quickly than by the hearing or inquiry methods. It is important that you read our booklet 'Making your planning appeal' about the various procedures used to determine planning appeals.

*Please tick **one** box only* ✔

1. **WRITTEN REPRESENTATIONS**   ☑

   Can the whole site be seen from a road or other public land <u>and</u> there is no need for the Inspector to enter the site (eg to take measurements or to enter a building)? If yes, please tick the box. If so, we will arrange an unaccompanied site visit.   ☐

2. **HEARING**   ☐

   Although you may prefer a hearing, we will decide whether a hearing is suitable for your appeal after consulting the LPA.

3. **INQUIRY**   ☐

   Please give reasons why you think an inquiry is necessary.

   _____

   _____

3

FIGURE 3.1 Appeal Form Cont...

J. ESSENTIAL SUPPORTING DOCUMENTS

**The documents listed in 1–6 below, must be sent with your appeal form; 7–10 must also be sent if appropriate.
If we do not receive all your appeal documents by the end of the 6 month appeal period, we will not deal with
it. Please tick the boxes to show which documents you are enclosing.**

                                                         ✔

1. A copy of the original **planning application** sent to the LPA. ☑

2. A copy of the **site ownership certificate and ownership details** submitted to the LPA
   at application stage (this is usually part of the LPA's planning application form). ☑

3. A copy of the **LPA's decision notice** (if issued). ☑

4. A **plan showing the site outlined in red**, including two roads clearly named
   (preferably on a copy of a 1:10,000 Ordnance Survey map). ☑

5. Copies of **plans, drawings and documents** sent to the LPA as part of the application. ☑

6. Any **additional plans, drawings and documents** sent to the LPA but which did not form part
   of the original application (eg drawings for illustrative purposes). ☐

Copies of the following must also be sent, if appropriate:

7. **Additional plans or drawings** relating to the application but not previously seen by the LPA.
   Please number them clearly and list the numbers here: ☐

   _____

8. Any relevant **correspondence** with the LPA. ☑

9. If the appeal is against the LPA's refusal or failure to grant permission for 'details' imposed on a grant of outline
   permission, please enclose:

   (a) the relevant outline application; ☐

   (b) all plans sent at outline application stage; ☐

   (c) the original outline planning permission; ☐

10. A copy of any Environmental Statement plus certificates and notices relating to publicity
    (if one was sent with the application, or required by the LPA). ☐

11. If you have sent other appeals for this or nearby sites to us and these have not been decided,
    please give details and our reference numbers. ☐

    _____

    _____

K. PLEASE SIGN BELOW

(Unsigned forms will be returned. Signed forms must be received by us within the 6 month time limit)

1. I confirm that I have sent a copy of this appeal form and documents to the LPA – **N.B.** _if you do not, your appeal
   will not normally be accepted._

2. I confirm that section J has been fully completed.

3. I will send 2 copies of any further documents relating to this appeal to the Inspectorate.

Signed _____ _Graham Buttfinch_ _____ (on behalf of) <u>RESIDENTIAL RENTALS</u>

                   G BUTTFINCH (DIRECTOR)   25TH JUNE 2001

Name (in capitals)_____   Date _____

5

OBJECTIONS

It's sometimes possible to negotiate with the people making appeals. Similar considerations apply as when approaching them about planning applications (see Chapter 2). The names and addresses of the appellant and agent are on the appeal form. If the appellant is willing and able to meet some or all of your objections you need to ensure the scheme is amended formally. A new planning application would be required for significant amendments. Sometimes a revised application can be approved before a decision on the appeal is made and ideally the appeal should be withdrawn by the appellant. Where amendments are relatively minor, revised drawings can be substituted in the appeal documents or conditions can be suggested. Bear in mind that whilst you, the appellant and the district council might agree on amendments and conditions, an inspector isn't compelled to do so. If you have any doubts about amendments, check with the planning officer.

Meeting the planning officer

The planning officer assigned to handle an appeal for the district council isn't necessarily the same officer who dealt with the planning application. Arrange to meet him to discuss the appeal and the basis of the district council's case. See where you agree and where you want to lay more emphasis. When you eventually put forward your views, avoid merely repeating what the planning officer says. That would carry little weight with the inspector. Although you might appear to be on the same side as the district council, don't assume too much. Planning officers might not make all the points you feel are important or place the same emphasis on them. You might, however, be able to alert the planning officer to some new point which has not been raised previously. Where you get involved in a public inquiry, it's worth co-ordinating your case with the planning officer's.

APPEALS BY WRITTEN REPRESENTATION

The timetable for written representations appeals is generally strict so you must post your letter or statement by the date specified (see Figure 3.2). Late letters are likely to be returned without being taken into account. Obtain a certificate of posting or use special delivery if you don't send your letter until close to the deadline.

Appeal Statements

Your only opportunity to influence the planning inspector in a written representations appeal is by a letter or statement. However, any letter you wrote to the council about the planning application will be read by the inspector and, if you've nothing to add, you needn't write again. As with letters of objection to planning applications, it's for you to decide what to say in your appeal statement and how much detail you want to go into, but the general guidelines for writing letters of objection given in Chapter 2 apply even more strictly to letters on appeals - if you want them to be really effective.

FIGURE 3.2 Timetable for an Appeal by Written Representations (England)

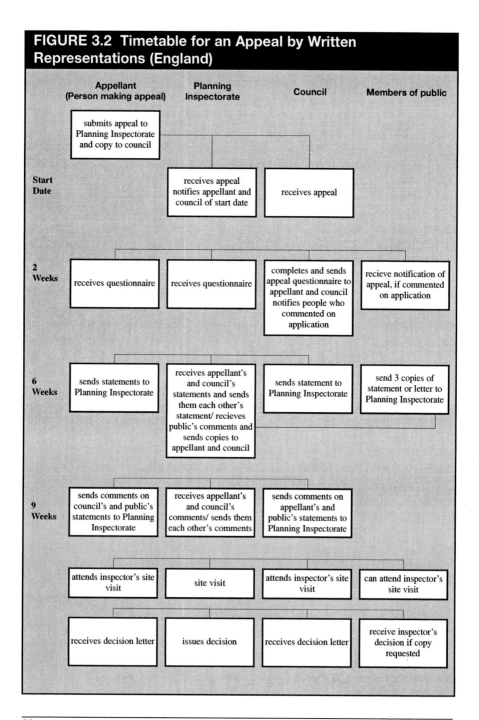

	Appellant (Person making appeal)	Planning Inspectorate	Council	Members of public
	submits appeal to Planning Inspectorate and copy to council			
Start Date		receives appeal notifies appellant and council of start date	receives appeal	
2 Weeks	receives questionnaire	receives questionnaire	completes and sends appeal questionnaire to appellant and council notifies people who commented on application	recieve notification of appeal, if commented on application
6 Weeks	sends statements to Planning Inspectorate	receives appellant's and council's statements and sends them each other's statement/ recieves public's comments and sends copies to appellant and council	sends statement to Planning Inspectorate	send 3 copies of statement or letter to Planning Inspectorate
9 Weeks	sends comments on council's and public's statements to Planning Inspectorate	receives appellant's and council's comments/ sends them each other's comments	sends comments on appellant's and public's statements to Planning Inspectorate	
	attends inspector's site visit	site visit	attends inspector's site visit	can attend inspector's site visit
	receives decision letter	issues decision	receives decision letter	receive inspector's decision if copy requested

If you've never seen a planning appeal inspector's decision letter, get hold of one for a similar case from a planning department and read it (see Figure 3.5). Adopt the same sort of format, style and content for your own statement. You might find it helpful to structure your appeal statement as follows: introduction; description; background; planning policy; and issues and conclusions.

Introduction

Head the appeal statement with the name of the proposed development, site address, application reference and appeal reference. Then mention anything significant that happened at the application stage that the appellant or council might have ignored. This might be discussions you had with the applicant for example, but avoid 'who said what and when' type descriptions. The inspector is interested in facts, not in arguments between the parties. State if you represent anyone else - neighbours, residents' association, amenity society or objectors group - what the body you represent is about and how many people you are speaking for.

Description

Inspectors only have a very short time to study the surrounding area, so set the scene by describing the locality. What you describe depends on the nature of the proposal and how wide its effects would be. Think about both physical appearance and use. For example, with an edge-of-town superstore, you might need to describe: the surrounding countryside because of the visual impact; the road network because of traffic generation; neighbouring houses because of disturbance; and the town centre and other shopping centres in, say, a 16 kilometre (10 mile) radius because of the effects on trade and their prosperity.

If you feel an area has a particular character, try to describe it. This is the sort of detail an inspector might not be able to pick up during a brief inspection. Draw attention to any special features that are relevant - historical associations, ancient buildings, rare wildlife species, or peculiarities of local architecture. The same applies to uses in the area - an old people's home or primary school nearby, a road used by horse riders or parents with children, or the number of takeaways already in the high street.

If you want to take the description of the area further you could carry out your own surveys. These needn't take long to do and, once collected, the information can be included in your text, shown in a table or marked on a map to support your arguments by providing tangible evidence. Where you're concerned about visual impact:

• travel around the area noting all the places where the site can be seen; take photographs; record what's seen around and near the site, what else the wider view contains, whether it would be screened and what it would be viewed against; try to establish how many people pass the viewpoint and would see the development
• judge what the effect of the proposal would be - it's not enough simply to say that it could be seen

FIGURE 3.3 An Appeal Plan

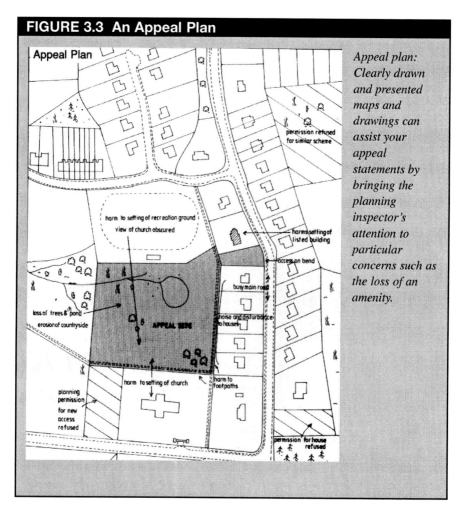

Appeal Plan

harm to setting of recreation ground / view of church obscured

permission refused for similar scheme

harm setting of listed building

access on bend

busy main road

noise and disturbance to houses

loss of trees & pond

erosion of countryside

APPEAL SITE

harm to setting of church

harm to footpaths

planning permission for new access refused

permission for house refused

Appeal plan: Clearly drawn and presented maps and drawings can assist your appeal statements by bringing the planning inspector's attention to particular concerns such as the loss of an amenity.

- consider showing all the viewpoints on a plan; pictures - photographs and plans - convey a great deal of information and get points across quickly

Where you're concerned about traffic levels:

- carry out a vehicle count; find a safe place where you can see the road clearly; using paper and pen, divide pages into columns and record separately half hour, one hour or morning and afternoon time periods; make a note of the date and time of start and finish
- pedestrian and other road user counts can be done in the same way

Where your concern relates to the loss of a use or over-provision of a use:

* carry out a land use survey; walk round the vicinity noting down what each building is used for, or just the uses you're interested in; if you're worried about losing housing in a town centre, count the buildings recently converted into offices or shops; if you're concerned about building on green open spaces, see how many are left and where they are, take photographs and compile a detailed list

Background

In this section of your statement, set out for the inspector any relevant circumstances or history. This can include planning decisions, although they are normally in the council's statement. Where you know, or can find out, the history of a site, include it if relevant, such as where an appellant tries to justify a proposal on the basis of existing levels of activity or the previous existence of buildings. Note any planning applications that have been permitted or refused before, and why. The planning officer's report on the original planning application often provides very useful summaries from which to extract information so use this information to guide your thinking and arguments in your statement. Ask the planning officer whether there are any other planning applications or appeals for similar proposals or in similar circumstances that might help you ascertain important issues and how they are dealt with. There are companies which can search computer records for other appeal decisions on the same type of development, location or issues (see Appendix II).

Planning policy

In deciding planning appeals, planning inspectors place more emphasis on government policy than do district councils. Your appeal statement needs to take this change in priorities into account, so ask the planning officer what government guidance is applicable to the case. Read through these guidance documents noting anything that relates to the appeal proposal, the title of documents and relevant paragraph numbers to quote in your statement. Then work through the Structure Plan, Local Plan and informal planning policy documents in the same way (see Chapter 1). Again, speak to the planning officer if you need advice on which policies apply. You might find it helpful to look back at what was said about planning policies in letters of objection to planning applications in Chapter 2.

Issues and conclusions

This is the section to express your opinions as persuasively as possible. State what you consider to be the main points, drawing on everything you've looked at, and reach conclusions based on that information. Say what's harmful about the proposed development and why, and what the consequences would be if it were to go ahead as proposed. Conclude your appeal statement by asking to be sent a copy of the inspector's decision letter. When your statement is complete, check you have the correct address for the Planning Inspectorate, or Planning Appeals Commission in Northern Ireland or Inquiry Reporters Unit in Scotland, and the correct appeal reference. Then take a copy for yourself and send off the required number of copies.

INSPECTORS' SITE VISITS

The site visit is the inspector's opportunity to see the appeal site, surrounding properties and area, and particular points mentioned in letters or statements. No discussion of the merits of the appeal takes place at site visits. In most cases, the appellant, or the appellant's representative, and a planning officer attend the visit, but where a site can be seen clearly from the road or other public land, an inspector is sometimes unaccompanied. Ask the planning officer to point out any specific physical features of the site, adjoining properties or locality that you feel the inspector should see. If you're not confident that this will be done as you'd want, you can ask in your appeal statement to be notified of the inspection so that you can attend - although in most cases, this should be unnecessary. About two months after the notice of appeal is submitted, double-check with the planning officer whether the inspection has been arranged.

INFORMAL HEARINGS

An informal hearing, as the name suggests, is supposed to be a discussion between an inspector and the parties in dispute of the contentious issues in a planning appeal and is on a smaller scale than a public inquiry. Appellants can be professionally represented and the planning officer usually represents the council but neither side has the same sort of professional team as at an inquiry. An informal hearing takes places after full written statements have been exchanged between the appellant and council.

You should write with your objections to the Planning Inspectorate in the same way as you would for a written representations appeal. Again, there's a strict timetable with which you must comply. It doesn't matter that you won't know at this stage which issues will be discussed at the hearing – include all your concerns. Where your points can be made adequately in writing, it's not essential to attend the hearing. However, being there gives you an opportunity to listen to the discussion, respond to what's said and reinforce points. If you do want to take part, say so in your letter/statement. It's better to attend and say very little than to miss the opportunity. Where a lot of people want to go along, it's possible that an inquiry would be held instead of an informal hearing.

Look at the appellant's and council's statements at the planning department and, if additional points occur to you, make a note of them to bring up at the hearing. You can attend the hearing regardless of whether you have written a letter. Let the planning officer know you intend to go along although the council should tell you the date and venue for the hearing anyway.

At the informal hearing the planning inspector explains the format and ascertains who is present before introducing the appeal, summarising the cases and outlining the areas he wishes to discuss. The inspector leads the discussion indicating in what order the parties are to speak and respond on the various issues he has identified. The inspector asks questions throughout but questioning by the parties isn't usually allowed and all comments and discussion is supposed to be directed to the inspector. You'll be given an opportunity to speak. Although the inspector will want to hear particularly about the issues he has defined, other points aren't excluded. The inspector will have your written comments, so don't just repeat these points at the hearing. The points made in the next section about speaking at public inquiries are also relevant here. To make a really effective contribution, you must have an understanding of the parties' cases beforehand as they'll be summarised only briefly by the inspector.

Discussion about the appeal is normally allowed to continue at the informal hearing site inspection. Thus it differs slightly from site visits for written representations and public inquiries in which those attending are confined to pointing out only physical features. Again, the inspector will lead the discussion at the site inspection.

PUBLIC INQUIRIES

A public inquiry is a formal hearing of a planning appeal before a member of the Planning Inspectorate, or in Northern Ireland the Planning Appeals Commission, or in Scotland the Inquiry Reporters Unit. It's held in a council's chamber or committee room, village hall or other similar public building and is like a very informal court hearing. A planning inspector presides at the front of the room, the appellant sits on one side and the district council opposite. Members of the public, including objectors, usually sit at the back of the room or in a public gallery (see Figure 3.4). An inquiry can last anything from a day to a number of months, the length depending on the scale and complexity of the proposal. Two or three days is common, however. The planning officer will be able to confirm whether there's to be an inquiry and how long it's programmed for. The council should notify you anyway if you objected to the planning application.

Before the inquiry, the council and appellant have to exchange pre-inquiry statements which set out the basis of their cases, the sort of evidence they intend to produce and which documents they'll refer to. The statements should be sent six weeks after the acknowledgement of the appeal. Both are available at the planning department, so use the information to help form your own case against the appeal. Note which arguments of the appellant you need to counter, and which areas of your own case need more work. Where objectors have a comprehensive or complex case and the funds available, a professional or professional team is often employed and the objectors can be made a 'party' to the appeal. This means they'll be more involved in the proceedings and treated similarly to the appellant and council. Like the other parties, a pre-inquiry statement might have to be exchanged. Any professionals employed by objectors must, therefore, have adequate knowledge of inquiry procedure and be suitably qualified.

Four weeks before the inquiry opens, the appellant and council (and objector if party to the inquiry) are supposed to exchange the full cases they intend to make. These

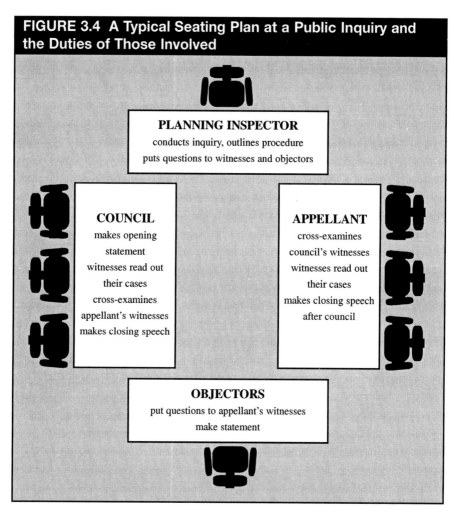

FIGURE 3.4 A Typical Seating Plan at a Public Inquiry and the Duties of Those Involved

PLANNING INSPECTOR
conducts inquiry, outlines procedure
puts questions to witnesses and objectors

COUNCIL
makes opening
statement
witnesses read out
their cases
cross-examines
appellant's witnesses
makes closing speech

APPELLANT
cross-examines
council's witnesses
witnesses read out
their cases
makes closing speech
after council

OBJECTORS
put questions to appellant's witnesses
make statement

documents, usually called 'proofs of evidence', are equivalent to their statements in a written representations appeal but usually far more detailed and thorough. Before going to the district council offices, you should first check their availability because planning officers are likely to be working on the appeal documents themselves. Make a note of the points you disagree with and any factual errors, recording the page and paragraph number for ease of reference later. You can write to the council with these points or arrange a meeting with the planning officer to discuss them in the hope the council will take them up. Alternatively you can deal with any points at the inquiry if you decide to speak. It's up to each inspector to decide who can participate - only the appellant, the council, owners/tenants of the land, and other planning authorities in the area have the absolute right to take part – but in practice, inspectors let members of the public speak. The notes you make working through the cases will also be useful as the basis of your questions to the witnesses if you're given that opportunity at the inquiry.

You are not, however, obliged to turn up or speak at the inquiry. You can, if you wish, attend the inquiry but not take part and just observe or just put your objections in writing in exactly the same way as for a written representations appeal.

Appellants, councils and objectors can use professional advisers to represent them at inquiries - barristers, solicitors, planning consultants, engineers, landscape architects and others. Any lawyers will act as advocates, leading the professional team. Other members of the team are known as expert witnesses and are 'called' in turn by the advocate to present their 'evidence' (their case) in the respective areas of expertise.

At inquiries, objectors, appellants and councils must be slightly cautious in what they say and do. Each party is expected to bear its own costs of taking part but if someone behaves 'unreasonably' at an inquiry he can become liable for another party's costs. 'Unreasonable' in this sense means recklessly causing another party to incur unnecessary costs at an inquiry. This could be, for example, turning up on the day of an inquiry with a 100 page report on an issue which hadn't previously been raised, or notified to the appellant in advance. It doesn't mean merely making a slight mistake or not being familiar with inquiry procedure. Unless you become fully involved in an inquiry, in which case professional help is advisable anyway, the risk of someone claiming costs against you, as an objector, is minimal. The inspector decides whether to award costs, which happens in less than 10% of appeals and about 80% of awards are against councils. If in doubt, speak to a planning officer.

Speaking at public inquiries

Attending and speaking at a public inquiry might seem daunting but it can give your objection more impact. Preparing your case for an inquiry is essentially the same as preparing a written representations appeal. Co-ordinate your efforts where you can; planning inspectors don't welcome a series of people all making the same point and probably wouldn't allow it. Contact with others at the planning application stage should point you to those likely to attend, and you can discover who else objects by looking at the council's file at the planning department. Decide whether you want to combine your representation at the inquiry or who'll make what points.

Arrange a meeting with planning officers to discuss presentation of cases, areas where you can support the council or points that would have more impact coming from you - for example, the existing effect of being next door to a development. If you've special knowledge, the council could call you as one of its witnesses.

Before you go to the inquiry make sure any notes and papers you take along are in good order and that all the points you'd like to raise are written down. On the first day of the inquiry, get to the venue in plenty of time, bringing with you all documents or drawings that you have for reference. If you want to submit anything new, such as supplementary statements, recent letters or additional plans you have drawn, take three or four extra copies of anything you haven't sent to the Planning Inspectorate. The appellant and district council should have extra copies of their cases to hand out at the inquiry, so ask for a copy if you've not managed to read it beforehand.

When the inquiry opens, indicate when asked by the planning inspector that you want to speak, or that you might do. If you can't attend the whole inquiry, tell the inspector at this point and he or she will usually arrange a convenient time for you to make your statement. It's up to the inspector whether objectors are permitted to put questions to witnesses. If it's allowed, you'll be invited to ask questions of each witness at appropriate moments, assuming you choose to do so. Do take advantage of the opportunity to put questions, as members of the public often ask far more pertinent and awkward questions of witnesses than the professionals. Here are some suggestions for putting questions:

- have a note of your questions in front of you
- try to order questions by grouping them in subjects or by following the order of the witness' case
- be ready to summarise the subject area of your questions in case the inspector asks where your line of questioning is leading
- ask specific questions, don't make statements - you have your chance to do this later
- don't go over precisely the same ground covered by previous questioners or the inspector will stop you
- be as concise and brief as possible
- stick to planning issues
- avoid highly technical points of law and procedure unless you are very confident of your ground

When the district council and appellant have presented their cases you have your chance to make a statement. As there are no particular formalities to observe just stand up and state your views simply and clearly. The inspector has to take a note of everything that's said so don't speak so quickly that the gist of your arguments can't be taken down. He should have a copy of any earlier objection you made in writing so if you've nothing new to add, don't repeat all the same material: just say that you're relying on your written objection, mention anything new that's come up and perhaps summarise in a few sentences two or three main points. Your statement should be the verbal equivalent of a letter of objection: the reasons why you object, who'll be affected and how, and what should be done (see Chapter 2). The difference at an inquiry is that the inspector will stop you (politely) if you waffle or introduce irrelevant facts. You might need to modify the original arguments you had already worked up in the light of what you've heard at the inquiry. Answers to cross examination questions might have thrown up interesting insights, which you can draw to the inspector's attention.

Be ready to answer questions about your views from the appellant and the inspector. Remember, the appellant might have a barrister skilled at leading witnesses down lines of thought and reasoning helpful to their client's case. This is what they're paid for after all but you shouldn't be asked technical planning questions unless you've gone into such matters in your case. The inspector will intervene if you're asked an unfair question. If you're subject to hostile cross-examination or find the barrister formidable, address your answers to the inspector, rather than to the questioner. Try not to get flustered: take your time to think about the question. Ensure your answers are consistent with your main arguments and with each other. If you don't know an answer say so. If you feel you're not qualified to deal with a particular question, again, say so.

The purpose of inquiries is to test the evidence. Don't rely on assertions you can't support or haven't thoroughly thought through. If you say a road is very dangerous, get police accident records. If you state a development will be visually damaging, know where you would be able to see it from.

Once all questions have been answered, the council sums up its case in a closing speech. The appellant then makes his closing speech. The inspector then makes arrangements for a formal site inspection and the inquiry closes. Objectors can ask to attend the site inspection but only do this if it's necessary for you to point out things referred to in your case. Check the inspector has a note of all important view points to visit: you can, for example, request the inspector views the site from your property. As with written representations appeals, discussion about the issues and merits of the proposal doesn't continue at the site inspection.

THE DECISION

Having heard all the evidence and completed his site inspection, the planning inspector writes a decision letter, or if the planning appeal is very large, controversial or legally complex, a report to the Secretary of State, Northern Ireland Department of the Environment, Scottish Executive or National Assembly for Wales. The length of time between site inspection and decision being issued varies depending on the complexity of cases; less than three or four weeks is unusual, six to eight weeks is more common. It can, for major development proposals, be many months.

Decision letters

The decision letter is sent to whoever made the appeal (that is, the appellant) and the council (see Figure 3.5). You should also receive the decision if you asked for a copy in your appeal statement or at the inquiry. Otherwise, you can see the decision or buy a copy at the planning department of the district council.

Appeals are either allowed or dismissed. Allowing or dismissing an appeal amounts to granting or refusing planning permission in the same way that district councils decide planning applications. This means that when appeals are allowed, conditions can be attached on design or use. If the application was for outline planning permission, the

FIGURE 3.5 Typical Appeal Decision Letter

Appeal Ref: T/APP/J7593/A/02/1347861
Pond Wood, Pheasant Lane, Spodge

The appeal is made by Paint Warz Limited against the decision of Hillton District Council.
The application (ref HA/01/2756) was refused by a notice dated 25th November 2001.
The development proposed is the use of land for paintball games and retention of a caravan for use as a changing room.

Summary of decision: The appeal is dismissed.

Main Issues
1. I consider that the main issues in this case are potential damage to the ecology of the wood, the impact on the wood's visual amenity and impact on adjoining houses.

Planning Policy
2. The Hillton District Local Plan was adopted in 1999. I have been referred to policies ENV5 and ENV7 concerning wildlife and landscape protection, and policy DOM8 regarding residential amenity. The appeal site is within the Green Hills Area of Outstanding Natural Beauty.

Ecology and visual amenity of the wood
3. The site comprises some 9 hectares of mixed deciduous native woodland known as Pond Wood. Pond wood as a whole is an attractive feature in the landscape, and within the wood are a number of important individual trees of great age and character, the subject of Tree Preservation Orders. The underlying soil of the wood is clay and I noted on my site visit the significant impact of pedestrian traffic, creating wide muddy paths. In addition to the paths, there are numerous makeshift structures used as cover by participants, in addition to the hut and caravan. These elements are conspicuous, especially when viewed from the public footpath. There is also evidence of damage to trees. In my view the use significantly detracts from the character of the wood and threatens preservation of its ecology, contrary to policies ENV5 and ENV7.

Impact on adjoining houses
4. I am concerned at the loss of amenity to adjoining houses, especially 'Woodside' which immediately adjoins the access and car park area. Traffic movements immediately adjoining the west flank wall of this dwelling would give rise to significant nuisance. The detailed representations from adjoining residents support my view that residential amenity would be significantly prejudiced were this appeal to be allowed.

Conclusions
5. I have, therefore, concluded that this appeal should not be allowed, since material harm would be caused to the Area of Outstanding Natural Beauty and to adjoining residents. I have considered all the other matters raised in the representations but I find none of sufficient weight to alter this conclusion.

Formal Decision
6. In exercise of the powers transferred to me, I hereby dismiss this appeal.

John Brightman
JOHN BRIGHTMAN BA DipTP MRTPI

inspector might make comments about the way the site should be developed, so read the decision letter carefully. What the inspector says beyond the actual decision itself, can affect future development proposals. Even if an appeal is allowed, a new planning application can be made for a variation or for something quite different.

When you have read the decision letter, discuss any implications and points that you don't understand with the planning officer. Appeals are sometimes dismissed for reasons which the appellant can overcome: for example, an inspector might say a site is suitable for development but the actual scheme put forward wasn't the right one. A dismissed appeal isn't, therefore, necessarily the end of the line. Any future planning applications will be judged against what the inspector says in his decision letter.

If a planning application is made for the same development on the same site within two years, in the absence of a change in circumstances, the council can refuse to process it. This stops applicants trying to wear down councils and objectors by making repetitive planning applications. Apart from this, there's nothing to stop new applications being made.

CHALLENGING APPEAL DECISIONS

Appeal decisions can be challenged in the courts within six weeks of the decision letter being issued. Decisions can only be challenged on legal grounds - that the inspector acted outside his authority or prejudice was caused by a failure to follow correct procedure. Decisions can't be challenged on their planning merits or matters of opinion. Out of all appeal decisions made, less than one in a hundred are challenged in the courts. Of those challenges, typically 20-30% are subsequently withdrawn, a similar proportion aren't defended on behalf of the Secretary of State, around 10% are turned down in court and 20-30% are upheld in court. When a court challenge does succeed, the appeal goes back to be re-decided by an inspector.

In most instances, leave the job of challenging appeal decisions in the courts, to the council. Consult a solicitor experienced in planning work before thinking about taking such a step yourself: you'd need to have funds running into many thousands of pounds to take an appeal decision to court.

COMPLAINTS

If you feel there was something wrong with procedure at an inquiry, you can complain to the Council on Tribunals and if you're unhappy with how you were treated by the inspector, you can write to the Complaints Officer at the Planning Inspectorate or in Northern Ireland, approach the Chief Commissioner at the Planning Appeals Commission or in Scotland, the Chief Reporter at the Scottish Executive Inquiry Reporters Unit.

The Ombudsman deals with unfair treatment through maladministration including failure to follow proper procedures. Complaints about district councils are researched by the Local Government Ombudsman (see Chapter 2) and those about central government departments including the DTLR, Northern Ireland DoE, Scottish Executive and Welsh

Assembly are investigated by Parliamentary Ombudsmen, but only at the request of a Member of Parliament. The Ombudsman has booklets about investigations so read these before deciding whether to make a complaint. The addresses of these bodies appear in Appendix II. Note that none of the above can question the merit of an appeal decision or change the result.

APPEALS - ACTION CHECK LIST

1   Check with the district council whether a planning appeal has been made.

2   Find out the date for submitting comments and the date of the inquiry or hearing (if there is going to be one).

3   Study the appeal documents and make notes.

4   Contact the planning officer to discuss the appeal and stay in touch to monitor progress.

5   Alert other potential objectors and the media.

6   Write your appeal statement and send it to the Planning Inspectorate, in Scotland to the Inquiries Reporters Unit or in Northern Ireland to the Planning Appeals Commission. Ask to receive a copy of the decision letter.

7   Read the statements by the council and appellant at the district council and write a further letter if new points arise.

8   Where an inquiry/hearing is to be held, prepare your case and attend.

9   Look at the planning inspector's decision letter.

We know that most development should have planning permission before being carried out - but what happens if it doesn't? This is one of the most vexed questions in the whole planning system. Members of the general public have an important role to play in spotting and alerting councils to unauthorised development. We therefore now look at what you can realistically do if you think development is taking place without permission or is breaking the conditions of a planning permission.

Nearby occupiers are often affected by activity such as vehicles arriving and leaving, lorries using an unsuitable access or visually damaging activity in the landscape. Alternatively, building work might start where you wouldn't expect to see it - in open countryside, close to your boundary or on a Listed Building. When you see something like this happening, you won't know whether it's authorised or not.

WHAT YOU CAN DO

The first thing to do is to get your facts straight, so telephone or visit the planning department and ask whether planning permission has been given or look up the planning record to see what planning permissions there might be. Even where permission exists, the development can still be breaking conditions or not being carried out as approved. If a planning application has been made, but not decided, follow the advice set out in Chapter 2. Where no planning permission exists and no application has been made, there are a number of steps you can take but don't put off action for too long. There are time limits on councils to take enforcement action (see page 84).

Apart from using the planning system, you might be able to take legal action yourself, depending on the circumstances. This could be where trespass is taking place, there's damage to your property, where statutory nuisance arises or a covenant in title deeds is breached. Speak to your Citizens Advice Bureau or solicitor about this. It's also possible for members of the public to initiate prosecution for unauthorised work to Listed Buildings.

If someone has carried out building work, is using a property or intends to carry out development, it's possible he or she has applied to the district council for a Lawful Development Certificate to establish whether the development is allowable without planning permission. This certificate states whether or not planning permission is legally needed for a development; it doesn't consider the merits of the development: for example, an application was made at Walton-on-Thames, Surrey to ascertain whether a tennis court with an underground triple garage below required a planning application. The council thought it did but, on appeal, the Secretary of State decided the proposal came within 'permitted development' rules and, therefore, no application was needed.

You could see an application for a Lawful Development Certificate advertised in the local paper or receive notification through the post. Councils don't have to publicise

FIGURE 4.1 An Example Planning Record Card

Crowdale District Council Planning Record Card
LAND SOUTH OF HOME FARM, CHURCH LANE

Ref no.	Description	Decision	Appeal
126/62	Use of land as caravan site	Granted 1/7/63	
485/65	Erection of office/toilets	Granted 4/11/65	
87/75	Extension of indoor sports area	Granted 9/3/75	
983/79	Outline, 15 houses	Refused 12/2/80	Dismissed 8/2/81
412/81	Change of use to farm shop	Granted 20/10/81	
756/87	Change of use to light industrial units	Refused 3/6/87	Allowed 2/3/88
1107/92	Erection of two new light industrial units	Granted 9/9/92	

A record of all planning applications and decisions made on a property is kept by the district council. Often there is a record card or sheet for each property.

these applications but often do as the history and existing use of a property is sometimes crucial to the council's decision. Evidence from local people can be especially important.

Contacting the developer

Apart from Lawful Development Certificates, there's usually no planning application when unauthorised development is being investigated so we use the term 'developer' here in place of 'applicant'. Developers could be private individuals, small businesses, site operators, farmers or builders.

When you suspect unauthorised development is occurring you could try discussing the development with the person responsible but discretion is needed. The type of person who ignores or flouts planning regulations, often where significant profit is at stake, isn't likely to warmly welcome outside interest. Better to go through official channels than to sour a relationship with a neighbour or get into an argument. Developers might be unaware permission is needed but most probably they are taking a chance, hoping no one notices. If they know you're aware of what they're doing and that you're prepared to take it farther, they might stop or be persuaded to make a planning application. Through friendly discussion you might be able to discover precisely what's going on and whether there's in fact unauthorised development at all. Discussion might result in activity being changed in a way which would make it acceptable to you. So much the better if this can be achieved without the need for an official complaint.

Meeting the planning officer

If a development still concerns you, contact the planning department which will point you to the officer you need to speak to initially. Tell him or her what activity is going on, when it started, who's doing it, where it's taking place, and why you're concerned. Take along any photographs, video tapes or records of activity you have collected. Ask the officer to investigate. Some district councils don't take action, except in more extreme cases, unless they receive a complaint, so you might be asked to put your complaint in writing. This should be kept confidential by the district council. The letter of complaint doesn't have to be a comprehensive statement: just set out briefly the facts you told the officer initially.

Following a complaint, officers look up the planning history and any planning permissions that exist. They'll visit the property and speak to the owner or occupier, and possibly to neighbours. Councils can serve notices on owners and occupiers to get more information about what's going on. The officers are then in a position to form a view on whether there is unauthorised development.

Contacting councillors

Where nothing happens after your initial complaint or there are long periods when no action seems to be taken, first establish with the planning department that the development you're concerned about is actually unauthorised and one that the council can potentially do something about. Then think about lobbying councillors. Your approach should be similar to that advised when seeking the support of councillors in opposing a planning application (see Chapter 2).

Development taking place without planning permission undermines councillors' powers of development control and they often seem as concerned about this aspect, as they are about the effects of the development itself. Tell the councillor what's happened, what you've done about it so far and ask him to look into the case. In most instances the councillor will ask an officer to investigate or for information about the case. Invite the councillor to visit the site so he can see the effects of the unauthorised development - disturbance, traffic, appearance or whatever. Failing this send photographs.

Unlike planning applications, where councils have to react to proposals, enforcement puts the onus on councils to initiate action. With competing pressures on officers, a bit of lobbying, and a councillor's strong support can get that action taken or move it up the list of priorities. Usually, a report on the unauthorised development will go to a planning committee so check with the planning department if it is and when. This can be a good point to urge a councillor to press for immediate action. You can attend the meeting and listen to the discussion but let the councillor you have lobbied know you are going to attend. Some unauthorised development cases are discussed by the committee in private.

Seeking support

If you're concerned by an activity going on without planning permission, other people are likely to be as well. As with planning applications, there's strength in numbers: the more people who complain and the louder they do so, the greater the likelihood that the council will act. Mobilise support by alerting other people and advising them what to do (see Chapter 2). Where the unauthorised development is small scale, it could only affect those in the immediate area. Even here, however, it might set a precedent which, if unchallenged, others could follow. This could then give it added significance. Where the history of the property is important, contacting other objectors might put you in touch with someone who knows about it in detail, which could be useful for your case and for the council's.

Contact the parish council, which will probably be concerned at the infringement of planning control, in addition to the development itself. Encourage parish councillors to contact the district council complaining about the development and urging prompt action.

WHAT COUNCILS CAN DO

Most councils have enforcement officers who investigate unauthorised development and complaints. They're not necessarily qualified planning officers but do have the support of the planning department behind them. An enforcement officer's role is often to collect information, which planning officers then weigh up and act upon.

Enforcement action

The various powers that councils possess to take action against unauthorised development are known collectively as enforcement. Enforcement is a controversial and difficult area, the subject of a great deal of litigation. The number of cases where formal action is taken by councils is around 15,000 a year. Here are some examples where action was taken:

- car boot sales taking place in the Green Belt at Averley, Essex
- a 3.3 metre (11 foot) deep hole dug in a garden at Hampstead Heath, London
- double glazing units put in a listed Queen Anne farmhouse at Downley, Buckinghamshire

Some uses seem prone to going ahead without planning permission - car breakers and scrap yards, waste disposal and transfer, and car repair and spraying. Often they're uses both very profitable and unpleasant to live near. In some instances there's no doubt that development is carried out flagrantly, with blatant disregard for planning controls. In others, considering the complexity of some planning law and grey areas of interpretation, it can happen quite innocently. Development that's not carried out exactly as approved in a planning permission or fails to comply with conditions on a planning permission can also be the subject of enforcement action.

It's not a criminal offence to carry out development without planning permission, but where a council takes action and the offender doesn't comply he can then be prosecuted.

FIGURE 4.1 An Example of Unauthorised Development

In this typical example of unauthorised development, poultry sheds and their surroundings were transformed into a builder's yard and crash repair works in which panel beating and paint spraying took place. Fifteen years after the uses began, the council had failed to stop the unauthorised development; appeals on this case went all the way to the House of Lords.

Fines of up to £20,000 can be imposed. However, work on Listed Buildings, Scheduled Ancient Monuments, Tree Preservation Order trees, and demolition in Conservation Areas, without the appropriate permission, is a criminal offence.

Members of the public can't take enforcement action themselves or insist that a district council does on their behalf, because district councils have discretion to decide on whether to act. Since this can be the cause of great frustration and bitterness to the public, we shall look at the reasons why councils sometimes don't, or can't, take enforcement action:

- the activity taking place might not come within the meaning of development for planning purposes (see Chapter 1)
- planning permission could've been granted by the council, or at appeal. Applicants usually have up to five years to carry out development and a planning permission, perhaps contentious when first approved, could've been renewed several times. If all conditions requiring approval of details, materials and landscaping are complied with, and the scheme goes ahead in line with the approved plans, there's little a council can do short of revoking planning permissions. This is a drastic step that can be very expensive as compensation is paid to the owner by the council
- development could be of a type allowed under the 'permitted development' rules in which the government, in effect, grants automatic planning permission for many types of building work and uses: everything from building a garage to holding stock car racing meetings (see Chapter 1). In certain circumstances councils take away these automatic rights (see Chapter 6) or approve only certain aspects of the development. More often, however, the 'permitted development' can just go ahead without anyone being notified
- apart from changes of use which come within the 'permitted development' regime, other changes are allowed without planning permission by government under its 'use classes order' (see Chapter 1). Thus no permission is needed for a building society to become a betting shop or a church an art gallery
- there are time limits for taking enforcement action so, if nothing's done within the specified times, councils can't take action afterwards. Such development is then said to be 'immune from enforcement'. The time limits are four years for building works and using any building to live in, and ten years for changes of use and breaking planning conditions
- as a matter of policy the government discourages enforcement action just because development is unauthorised. When planning rules are infringed, councils are supposed to act only in situations where they wouldn't grant planning permission, or not without conditions. Even if a council doesn't itself like a development, it must take into account whether it would be given permission at appeal. If it would, the council is unlikely to take action.

These then are the legitimate planning reasons why councils might not do anything about unauthorised development. There could, of course, be other non-planning reasons why they don't (see Chapter 1).

When you make a complaint to the council, the planning officer should let you know the outcome of these investigations. If they conclude there's nothing the council can do, they should explain why. If you're not satisfied with their response, think about getting separate professional advice for confirmation.

Enforcement procedure

Where an unauthorised development is harmful, planning or enforcement officers can contact developers and try to persuade them either to stop what they're doing or to make a planning application. If the developer does neither, the planning officer writes a report, which is put on an agenda for a planning committee meeting. Sometimes reports on delicate enforcement cases and discussion about them aren't made public. The planning committee decides whether to authorise officers to take enforcement action. Often, a committee delays taking such a decision until all other avenues are exhausted and meanwhile asks officers to negotiate with the developer. Beyond staying in touch with planning or enforcement officers to keep abreast of events, there's little you can do within the enforcement procedures at this stage.

In most cases, an enforcement notice is served on the owner and occupier requiring the activity to cease, the land to be returned to its former condition, buildings to be demolished or some other remedy (see Figure 4.3). The notice says how long the council gives the developer to carry out what he's been required to do. A council can, however, only take action against the part or aspect of the development that infringes planning rules: for example, a horticultural business at Tarleton, Lancashire was selling produce grown both on site and bought in from elsewhere. Agricultural businesses are allowed to sell their own produce, so enforcement action taken by the district council was only against the sale of items bought in for re-sale.

If a council also serves a stop notice, the unauthorised activity must cease straight away. These are used very rarely as compensation can be claimed by developers if councils get their facts wrong or make mistakes in procedure.

A person who receives an enforcement notice can appeal against it (within 28 days), comply with it, or ignore it. The latter course is likely to land him in court. Prosecution is something only the council can do. If the developer complies, that should be the end of the matter as the notice continues to have effect. A watchful eye might be needed to check activity doesn't recur in the future. If it does, contact the planning department again and tell them what's happening. You could take photos to support your contentions. A developer who doesn't comply with an enforcement notice can be prosecuted, but going to court is expensive and time consuming, so a council is inevitably reluctant to take this step. It might be months before a council takes formal action, especially where unauthorised development does not threaten life, limb and public safety.

FIGURE 4.3 A Council's Powers of Enforcement Against Unauthorised Development

Planning Contravention Notice

Used to find out what's happening at properties where there might be unauthorised development. Served on owners, occupiers and operators with 21 days to respond. Notice asks about: types of activities going on; when they began; names and addresses of owners, occupiers and operators; any existing planning permissions; and any reasons why planning permission isn't needed.

Enforcement Notice

Used to stop or remedy unauthorised development that's already taken place. Served on owners, occupiers and anyone else affected. States the unauthorised development, what must be done about it, and in what time. Comes into effect after 28 days, unless an appeal is made.

Stop Notice

Used only with enforcement notice. Stops unauthorised development before enforcement notice comes into effect or while an appeal is running. Councils liable to pay compensation for loss or damage caused if notice withdrawn or mistakes over facts or procedure made. Used where a developer knew planning permission was needed, refuses to make planning application, and is causing severe harm.

Breach of Condition Notice

Used where condition on planning permission that's carried out isn't complied with. States what conditions are concerned, what must be done to comply, and within what period. No appeal, can only be challenged in magistrates court.

Injunctions

Used where serious and irreversible harm would be caused. Issued by High Court or County Courts using their discretionary powers. Stops unauthorised activity starting or continuing.

Section 215 Notice

Used to get untidy land and buildings cleaned up. Doesn't apply to untidiness caused in ordinary course of lawful activity. Served on owners and occupiers. Sets out what steps must be taken and gives time limit of at least 28 days. No appeal, can only be challenged in magistrates court.

APPEALS AGAINST ENFORCEMENT

About 4,000 enforcement appeals are made every year; about a third of these are later withdrawn. Of those decided at appeal, very roughly a third of enforcement notices are upheld (supported), one third are quashed (not supported), and in the remainder of cases the enforcement notice is only partially successful. The various specified grounds for appealing against enforcement notices include that the development doesn't need planning permission, the alleged activity isn't taking place and that planning permission for the development ought to be granted anyway. The issues disputed in an enforcement appeal can be about facts, legal opinion and planning merits. An appeal against an enforcement notice is, in practice, similar to an appeal when planning permission has been refused. Like a planning appeal it can be decided by written representations, informal hearing or public inquiry. You have all the same opportunities to influence the decision. The most effective way to deal with appeals is described in Chapter 3.

Where an appeal against an enforcement notice is made, the unauthorised development can continue. There might, however, be practical reasons why a developer wouldn't carry on, such as the possibility of having to demolish or restore buildings, but only the council serving a stop notice or getting a court injunction, can bring an authorised development to an immediate halt.

An applicant can also appeal if he disagrees with a council's decision on an application for a Lawful Development Certificate. The basis for these appeals is only that planning permission isn't needed, and here the arguments are about fact and the law, but not about planning merits.

Enforcement appeal statements

For both enforcement and Lawful Development Certificate appeals, confirm with the planning officer what issues are going to be relevant. This depends on the precise nature of the application and on the grounds on which the developer appeals. At the same time find out what the council is going to do itself and ask whether there's any information the officer thinks you could usefully provide to help the council with its case. Make sure what you propose to do is going to be relevant to the decision. If you know about the property - possibly because you live or work nearby - the officer might ask whether you'd be prepared to give evidence if an inquiry is being held. Also check the time scale for submitting your comments and confirm the application reference and address to send comments to.

Look back to Chapter 2 for guidance on drawing up a letter or statement to send to the Planning Inspectorate. For both enforcement and Lawful Development Certificate appeals concentrate on factual evidence to show why the development is harmful. Contrast the situation before, with the situation afterwards. You can collect valuable information about an unauthorised use by observation of the site (see Chapter 3). If you decide to do this, think very carefully about your personal safety; don't put yourself in danger. Planning officers sometimes have police escorts when serving enforcement notices and going on to sites.

In your enforcement appeal statement, include a request to receive a copy of the decision letter. Once your letter or statement is complete, copy it and send the required number of copies to the Planning Inspectorate, remembering to show the appeal reference clearly. If a public inquiry or informal hearing is to be held, follow the steps set out in Chapter 3.

THE DECISION

An enforcement appeal decision letter is similar to one for a planning appeal. Depending on the circumstances, the planning inspector or Secretary of State (or equivalent) decides whether planning permission is needed, whether the enforcement notice is valid and, where the appellant has argued that permission should be given, whether to grant planning permission. Where enforcement action is upheld on appeal, the decision letter can vary the amount of time given to remedy the unauthorised development. When an enforcement notice comes into effect after an appeal, the situation is the same as described earlier in this Chapter under 'Enforcement procedure'.

If a council doesn't act properly or effectively in dealing with a case of development without planning permission, you can complain to the Local Government Ombudsman (see Chapter 2).

UNAUTHORISED DEVELOPMENT - ACTION CHECK LIST

1   Check with the district council whether planning permission is needed.

2   Speak to a planning or enforcement officer about unauthorised development.

3   Contact the developer.

4   Contact the parish and district councillors.

5   Alert other potential objectors and the media.

6   Write a letter of complaint to the district council.

7   Monitor the council's action and progress.

8   If there is an appeal, write an enforcement appeal letter or statement and send it to the Planning Inspectorate, Inquiries Reporters Unit or Planning Appeals Commission.

9   Where an inquiry is to be held, prepare for it and attend.

10 Look at the inspector's decision letter.

11 Check the unauthorised development does not recur.

Local Plans are the district council's blueprint for the future of your village, town, city and area. The policies they contain touch your life every day. If you want a say in the future of your environment and community, you need to get involved in the Local Plan-making process. Your actions at this stage can be more effective than trying to stop or influence planning permission later, because planning applications and appeals are decided by reference to Local Plans. By influencing the content of these plans, you can help set the criteria for planning decisions. Don't assume that councils will look after your interests when preparing their Local Plans – it's up to you to make your views known. Developers and landowners are becoming increasingly involved in Local Plan preparation: so should you.

The pattern and type of development throughout the United Kingdom is determined through the plan-making process. In most of England, county councils draw up county-wide Structure Plans and in Scotland groups of councils collaborate to produce Structure Plans. These plans contain general policies for development - areas for expansion, areas for restraint and overall amounts of commercial, industrial and residential building, and so on. The district council or individual Scottish council prepares a more detailed Local Plan for the whole of its area, within the framework provided by the respective Structure Plan. Districts in Northern Ireland also prepare Local Plans. In Wales and in English Metropolitan areas and a few other areas in England, councils prepare a single plan, called a Unitary Development Plan, which incorporates both strategic and detailed planning policies. For convenience, references to 'Local Plan' should be read to include Unitary

Development Plans and whatever type of council you have, it's expected to have a district-wide Local Plan. In theory, Local Plans are supposed to cater for a 10-year period and should be reviewed every five years but, in practice, they're reviewed at irregular intervals, depending on pressures for change and the available resources of the district council. Typical chapter headings and content of a Local Plan are shown in Figure 5.1.

GETTING INVOLVED

Bearing in mind their fundamental importance to everyone living, working or owning property in an area, it's surprising how few people are aware of the existence of Local Plans. Although district councils publish notices in local papers, issue press releases and hold exhibitions and display information at the planning department, it's easy to miss the publicity about Local Plans. Your parish council and local conservation and amenity groups, as well as other local groups who might be interested, are informed about the plans being drawn up. If you're part of a group who want to comment on a Local Plan, register your interest with the council. The best bet though, if you don't want to miss the opportunity to influence the policies which affect you and your community, is to contact the Local Plan section of the planning department at your district council. Ask whether there's an adopted plan or whether one is being prepared and what stage it's reached. Make sure you fully understand the answer as the Local Plan process is complicated. There might still be more than one Local Plan covering the district and these could be at different stages in the process.

If there are one or two issues or particular sites you're interested in, mention them and ask how they're affected by Local Plan preparation. Arrange to meet a planning officer if you're in any doubt. Where you're concerned about the possibility of mining, quarrying or waste disposal, contact the county council for information about the relevant plans. The Local Plans officer should be able to indicate when a plan being prepared is likely to be published for public comment. Ask him to notify you when a plan reaches a stage where you can comment. For your contribution to have maximum impact, it's essential that you find out the dates for submitting your comments and objections as early as possible. Meanwhile, stay in touch with the planning department to keep abreast of progress. Alternatively, if you think you might eventually get professional help, get a planning consultant to monitor Local Plan progress for you.

When councils have worked up a first draft Local Plan, it's approved by the planning committee for publication. A plan at this stage is called a 'first deposit draft' or 'consultation draft'. This the council publicises to get public reaction and invites consultees to make representations about the plan. There's no set period for this stage, although it's at least six weeks. Councils consider feedback and a revised plan, drawn up by planning officers, is approved by councillors. The plan is then published as a 'deposit draft'. In this slightly more formal stage in the procedure, a plan is put on deposit for six weeks, during which anyone can make comments. Again, councils take steps to involve the public and get reactions from consultees. A statement about publicity, public participation and consultation is also available from the council.

FIGURE 5.1 Topics Covered by Local Plans

Introduction
- Plan preparation
- Relationship with other plans
- Plan purpose and objectives
- Monitoring and review of plan

Housing
- Policy context
- Amount and location of new housing
- Housing needs
- Conversions and changes of use
- Special needs
- Design and environment

Employment
- Assessment of need
- Amount and location of office and industrial development
- Business areas
- Commercial development in the countryside
- Small businesses
- Relocating badly sited industry

Shopping
- Existing shopping centres
- Amount, type and location of shopping development
- Local and neighbourhood shops
- Maintaining town centres
- Retail warehouses and superstores
- Access for disabled

Built environment and conservation
- New development and redevelopment
- Extensions and alterations
- Trees and open space
- Shop fronts and advertisements
- Conservation Areas
- Listed Buildings
- Protecting archaeological remains

Countryside
- Development restraint outside built-up areas
- Development in Green Belts and Areas of Outstanding Natural Beauty
- Landscape improvement
- Rural housing and employment
- Agriculture and agricultural buildings
- Nature Conservation and Sites of Special Scientific Interest

Highways and Transportation
- New roads
- Road improvements
- Parking standards
- Town centre traffic management
- Facilities for public transport
- Highways and new development

Recreation, tourism and leisure
- Provision of sport and leisure facilities
- Uses in the countryside
- Holiday accommodation
- Tourist attractions
- Playing fields
- Country parks
- Amusement arcades

Utilities and community services
- Public utilities - gas, water, electricity, drainage, post office, telecommunications
- Schools and education
- Health facilities
- Community facilities
- Libraries

Comments on the deposit draft are classified as objections, which are against some aspect of the plan, or representations, which support some aspect of the plan. We'll generally refer to both as 'objections' in this chapter as similar considerations apply.

Studying a Local Plan

Once you ascertain that a Local Plan is being published, track down a copy at the district council office, parish council office or local libraries, or buy one from the district council. Read the introduction and summary, if there is one, to help set the scene for you. Next, look at the index. Assuming you don't want to read the whole plan cover to cover, turn to the issues which interest you and read those sections. There's often some overlap so do go through it carefully to avoid missing something important. Look at the proposals map, together with its key, to get an overview of the main land classifications. If it's a particular area or site you're concerned about, find it on the proposals map or inset map and see if it's allocated for a use or designated in some way. Make a note and look up relevant policies in the written part of the plan.

Where you're worried about certain types of development, or even specific development proposals, see how the policies of the plan affect them. There could be loopholes to close or new policies to suggest, to stop that development in future. Study how the plan deals with issues that concern you: policies might be weak, inappropriate or there might not be a policy dealing with a particular point. You can object to a plan on the basis that it omits policies that ought to be in there.

As you study the plan, write down points that occur to you as well as policy and paragraph numbers for future reference. If you don't understand any part of the plan, ask to speak to one of the planning officers as they're usually helpful and will clarify uncertainties for you.

Meeting the planning officer

Although there are specific periods in the Local Plan process for making representations and formal objections, there's nothing to stop you discussing the plan with a planning officer at any time. Even where a plan has been finalised recently, suggestions should be noted by the district council and taken into account later. In many ways it's a good idea to get in an early comment to sow the seeds for the future. The further the plan is advanced, the more entrenched the officers' views are likely to be. Because the plan can't actually be altered until it's formally reviewed, this might also affect the degree of interest shown by the officers.

When a Local Plan is published you can arrange to meet a planning officer or speak on the telephone. Mention your concerns and how you feel the plan might be improved, using your notes to back up your arguments. Listen carefully to the district council's views but don't be put off points you feel strongly about, without good reason. A draft plan contains the policies that the planning officers think are right for the area; naturally, they have a tendency to defend them. Use the information you get from the planning

FIGURE 5.2 Example Local Plan Insert Map

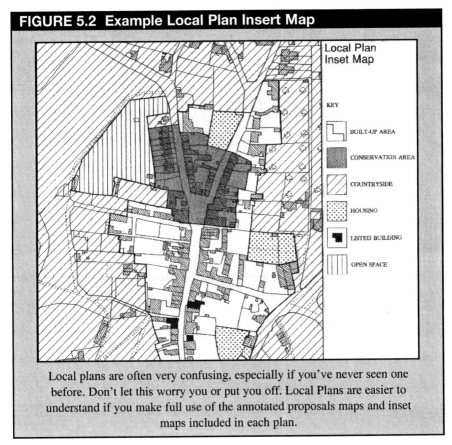

Local plans are often very confusing, especially if you've never seen one before. Don't let this worry you or put you off. Local Plans are easier to understand if you make full use of the annotated proposals maps and inset maps included in each plan.

officer to refine your views on the plan. Don't withdraw your objection unless you have firm guarantees that the plan will be amended. It's better to maintain your objection and explain what agreement has been reached in your objection form or statement than risk losing out and not achieving any results.

Once you're involved in the plan, you should be told of any modifications relevant to your objections, or you can get in touch with the officers periodically to keep up to date. Lists of proposed modifications are drawn up and published. You can inspect these at the planning department.

Lobbying councillors

Ultimately, it's the elected council members who decide what goes in the Local Plan and so it's they who must be influenced. Councillors set the tenor of the plan and what issues it must address, while planning officers carry out the technical side of Local Plan preparation. Councils set up sub-committees or working parties to oversee Local Plans.

Find out the names of the relevant councillors from the planning department. Before approaching councillors, bear in mind the main stages at which they have to make decisions (see Figure 5.3):

- forming initial ideas
- approving a first deposit or consultation draft
- considering comments and approving a revised deposit draft
- reacting to objections
- considering the Local Plan inquiry inspector's report and planning officers' suggested modifications to it
- adopting the plan

These are all opportunities for lobbying councillors to influence the Local Plan. For general comments on contacting councillors refer to Chapter 2. As with planning officers, it can be very worthwhile approaching councillors as early as possible - before anything is published - as the council is supposed to reflect the demands of people in the area. If there are particular issues such as types of development, areas that need protecting, traffic problems that you feel something should be done about, draw these to a councillor's attention. Write or meet them at routine weekly surgeries or ask them to attend a meeting of your group.

Councillors can themselves be objectors to the Local Plan: they might object to part of the plan that affects their own area. They can also agree to represent residents or interested groups at a Local Plan inquiry: for example, at the Nuneaton and Bedworth Borough Plan inquiry, individual objectors to a 52 hectare (128 acre) housing site had difficulty in co-ordinating their action so a councillor helped by acting as their advocate. Drawing up Local Plans takes years and council elections will occur during this period, so use this as an opportunity to secure councillors' support for your ideas.

Lobbying consultees

When Local Plans are made available for public inspection, they're also sent to a wide variety of national and local organisations for comment. The council issues a list of who was consulted at the time the Local Plan is put on deposit so check the list to make sure all groups or bodies you think might be interested were consulted and take their addresses to contact as potential supporters.

In most cases, it's not appropriate to contact what we might call technical consultees, like government advisory bodies and public utilities. However, if your concerns relate specifically to one or more of these bodies, you can contact them direct. Find out the appropriate department in the organisation, discuss your concern and see what they say. Their response could change your tack slightly or back up your arguments when you put your case forward. Speaking to consultees could possibly result in them looking at the plan again in the light of your particular concern.

FIGURE 5.3 Preparing a Local Plan

Stages of preparation	Opportunities for action by general public
Draft plan District council draws up draft proposal and planning policies	Discuss your concerns and views on development with councillors and planning officers
1st Deposit Draft plan published, sent to official consultees and publicised in the area	Submit comments to council and lobby councillors
Plan revised Comments and representations considered, plan altered and approved by councillors	
Deposit and objections Deposit plan published and publicised, objections and supporting representations submitted in minimum 6 week deposit period	Submit objection/representation form and lobby councillors
Negotiation and modifications Planning officers try to overcome objections and put forward modifications to the plan	Discuss objection with planning officers
Local Plan inquiry Inspector hears council's and objectors' cases	Draw up statement and/or speak at the inquiry
Inspector's report Report sent to council, which decides what changes to make	Lobby councillors
Modifications and objections Inspector's report and council's proposed modifications to the plan published, objections submitted in minimum 6 week period, council considers objections	Submit fresh objection/modification
Further inquiry If necessary, inspector hears objections to modifications and reports to council	Draw up fresh statement and/or speak at the inquiry
Plan adopted Council publicises intention to adopt plan formally and after 28 days votes to adopt, when it becomes a statutory plan	

Other objectors

So far, when we've talked about other objectors we mean other people who, like you, oppose a development. With Local Plans the situation is more complex: other objectors fall into two camps - those who share your views and those who want to change a plan in a way which you feel will be harmful. Just as you might object to aspects of a Local Plan, so developers and land owners certainly will, but their objectives will be to get land they own allocated for development, to remove or modify policies that restrict development and to secure new road links or other facilities which would be to their advantage. This sort of Local Plan objector is the equivalent of the applicant, appellant or developer in previous chapters. We look first at getting support from people who share your views about a plan.

Getting support

Similar considerations apply to objecting to a Local Plan as to objecting to a planning application. The more people who object to a particular policy or land allocated for development, the greater the chance that notice will be taken. To mobilise support for your objection do all the things that are set out in Chapter 2.

Objections and representations made at the deposit stages are available for the public to see at the district council planning department so you can find out whether anyone else objects to the same policies as you. Try contacting them to talk about the issues. See whether there's common ground and discuss taking action together. Their names and addresses will be on the formal objection forms.

When trying to enlist support from neighbours, local traders, businesses or whoever, don't expect them to know about the plan or its contents. You'll probably have some educating to do. Your main objectives here are to get people to write to the council when the consultation draft is published and to object to the plan when it goes on second deposit. Make sure people know the dates for submitting their comments. In any publicity material explain why the plan is important and which aspects of it are unsatisfactory. The Local Plan process is long and tedious for all but the truly dedicated. Objection fatigue can set in. If others, or indeed you, aren't able to do anything else, just concentrate on the two main objectives: write a letter or complete a form at the consultation stage and complete a form at the deposit stage.

The benefit of Local Plan preparation being a drawn-out business is that you do have time to organise support for your objection. Where there's sufficient support to form an action group or committee, you can launch a concerted campaign and possibly raise money to fund professional representation at the public inquiry. Alternatively, you can represent other objectors yourself, which means your written statement and speaking at the inquiry can be done on behalf of many people. Otherwise, decide in advance who's going to deal with which issue - effect of traffic, impact on landscape, effect on your properties and so on. The inspector is unlikely to let a string of objectors stand up and make exactly the same points, or to ask the planning officers similar questions. Good planning arguments are what the inspector is looking for, not weight of numbers. We look now at the other sort of Local Plan objector - ones who want to change a plan in a way you don't agree with.

Adverse objections

Countering objections you don't agree with can be difficult and technically complicated because, in theory, it isn't possible to object to another objection. The district council draws up its plan, the public, including developers, can object to it. The objector and the council argue on the merits of both the plan and the objection then the Local Plan inspector makes recommendations on those relative merits. An objection, therefore, isn't like a planning application or appeal where the views of the public are sought.

In practice, a representation in support of the relevant draft Local Plan policy is made to counter someone else's undesirable objection. If an objection throws up some new point or issue, you can object to the plan on the basis that it should include a policy on that matter or that a proposed policy should be strengthened. Making an objection puts you in a stronger position at the inquiry because objectors have the right to speak.

Countering adverse objections can also be tricky because you might not know what objections are made until the plan reaches the deposit stage. Even then, unless you check what's submitted during the six week objection period, you won't find out about objections made by others. It's easy to miss a controversial proposal put forward by a developer or other body. A common tactic used by developers is to submit objections right at the end of the deposit period for this reason. The best that can be done is to check with the planning officers as often as you reasonably can. As there'll be hundreds of objections, the officer might not be able to help unless it's something very specific you're concerned about, like one piece of land. Therefore, if you can, go to the planning department and ask to look at objections at the end of the objection period. Speak to an officer if you're not clear about any objections. If an adverse objection is made, get a written representation submitted quickly. The council usually welcomes support for the plan in the face of an objection that it will be fighting.

Once you establish someone has made an objection you want to oppose, you could speak to the person or organisation who made it but, as with planning applications, if you're fundamentally against what objectors put forward there's probably little point in contacting them. Whilst there's little for objectors to lose by pursuing an objection vigorously, they usually prefer not to be opposed by members of the public and so can be prepared to talk. If objectors are willing to discuss their cases, you might be able to agree concessions. In this event, ensure their objections are formally modified which can be done by the objector writing to the district council or at the Local Plan inquiry.

MAKING YOUR OBJECTIONS

Of the two main stages in the process for making comments to the council on a Local Plan, the first deposit or consultation draft is where the council is looking for feedback on its ideas. Public pressure is more likely to be effective here than later because the council's proposed policies won't be quite so firmly entrenched. Weight of numbers has a far greater effect on councillors than on a Local Plan inspector. On the other hand, the deposit draft is the more formal part of the procedure. This is your opportunity to challenge the council's views, with the Local Plan inspector to judge the planning merits of the case.

First deposit or consultation drafts

When the plan is published it'll contain information on when and where to make comments. There might be a simple form that you can use or, if you prefer, write a letter. If you want to put forward a comprehensive case now, there's nothing to stop you. Otherwise, all you need do is write to the council. In this letter you should:

- give the name of the plan
- identify the parts or policies you object to
- say briefly why you object
- set out what additions or changes you want to see

This letter will be read by planning officers and reported to councillors with all other comments. Remember, encourage as many people as you can to write at this stage. It doesn't necessarily take an enormous number of letters to influence the council. For example, a site was allocated for commercial development in the consultation draft Wrexham Maelor Local Plan. Around 25 letters opposing the allocation persuaded the borough council to take it out when the plan was revised.

Deposit drafts

Formal objections (against some aspect of the plan) or representations (supporting some aspect of the plan) must be made while the Local Plan is on deposit (see Figure 5.4). If you want to seek professional advice on a Local Plan, this is the time to do so (see Appendix I). Your consultant should fill in any forms on your behalf.

If you prefer to make your own objections or representations, fill in the Local Plan objection form provided by the district council (see Figure 5.5). If you object to more than one aspect of the plan, you're usually asked to use a separate sheet for each objection. There are no dire consequences if you complete this official looking form; objecting to a Local Plan isn't a legalistic business. The process is there to allow members of the public to get involved, and you're not committing yourself to anything further.

On the form fill in the policy reference and related paragraph numbers of the policy you object to or support (you should have a note of these from when you studied the plan). Remember, you can object on the basis that the plan should include additional policies and this puts you in a stronger position than just making a representation in support of the plan as it is. In this event, say you object to the failure of the plan to include a policy on whatever subject it is and suggest which section of the plan it should go into. Then decide whether a written case will suffice or whether you would prefer to take part in the Local Plan inquiry. Look back to Chapter 3 to get an idea of what an inquiry is like. Where your arguments are complex or need explanation and discussion, opt for the inquiry. If you're not sure, opt for the inquiry anyway as you can revert back to just a written statement later, if you change your mind.

FIGURE 5.4 Procedure for Objecting to a Local Plan on Deposit

Submit objection	complete form, send to council during 6 week deposit period
Acknowledgement	council writes confirming receipt of your objection
Report to committee	planning officers write a report on your objection to the council's committee and council decides whether to modify plan
Modifications	you are told if the council proposes modifications relevant to your objection
Questionnaire	council sends form asking how you want to support your objection
Pre-inquiry meeting	council appoints Programme Officer to administer inquiry Planning Inspectorate appoints inspector to hold inquiry meeting held for inspector to discuss inquiry arrangements with council and objectors
Objection statements	you send a statement of your case to the council council sends you its statement on your objection copies of both statements sent to the inspector
Inquiry programme	you are sent a timetable showing when you are due to present your objection at the inquiry
Inquiry	inspector hears your objection and council's case
Inspector's report and council's proposed modifications	council sends you the relevant extract from inspector's report and recommendation, and a statement on whether plan is to be modified
Objections to modifications	complete form, send to council during 6 week objection period objections resolved with or without another inquiry

Whatever you say on the form about appointing someone to act as your agent doesn't stop you deciding to get help later on. If you've agreed to represent other objectors, they should put your name here. There's often a question about working together with people who object to the same policies as you. Unless you've a particular reason for not doing so, answer 'yes' since this doesn't commit you to anything or restrict what you can do.

The most important part of the form is the section dealing with your reasons for objecting or supporting. This is the equivalent of grounds of appeal for a planning appeal

FIGURE 5.5 A Typical Local Plan Objection Form

Form for objecting to, or supporting

MARLBOROUGH DISTRICT LOCAL PLAN

For official use
Obj/Rep No:
Category:
Ack:

Question 1

Name and address

WOODSIDE RESIDENTS ASSOCIATION
C/O D. MILTON, MAY COTTAGE, COMMON LANE
WOODSIDE

Telephone No (home)   273 2715   **(work)**   681 4444

Question 2

Which policy did you object to or support?
1. POLICY DP/IS - ALLOCATION OF LAND AT WOODSIDE DEVELOPMENT.
2. FAILURE OF THE PLAN TO INCLUDE TRAFFIC MANAGEMENT POLICY FOR WOODSIDE.
3. POLICY TR29 - DEVELOPMENT ON WOODSIDE LANE.

Are you objecting   [✔]   or supporting   [ ]

Question 3

Do you want your objection to be either
a) considered in written form by the inspector   [ ]
OR
b) discussed at a public local inquiry   [✔]

Question 4

Have you appointed someone to act as your agent?   Yes [ ]   No [✔]
If yes, please give agent's name and address

Telephone No

Question 5

If others have objected to the same policy, would
you be willing to co-operate with them to present a
joint case at the public local inquiry?   Yes [✔]   No [ ]

FIGURE 5.5 A Typical Local Plan Objection Form cont...

Question 6

Please state here the full grounds on which your objection or representation in support is made

1.   LAND ALLOCATED AT WOODSIDE IS NOT SUITABLE FOR DEVELOPMENT.
IT WOULD BE DAMAGING TO THE LANDSCAPE AND HARMFUL TO WILDLIFE
HABITATS.
IT WOULD REDUCE THE NARROW GAP OF COUNTRYSIDE BETWEEN LAKESIDE
AND WOODSIDE.
WOODSIDE LANE IS NOT SUITABLE AS AN ACCESS ROAD.

2.   THE PLAN SHOULD CONTAIN A POLICY FOR TRAFFIC MANAGEMENT IN
WOODSIDE. ROADS IN WOODSIDE ARE USED AS A THROUGH ROUTE FOR
TRAFFIC COMING OFF THE MAIN ROAD. THIS IS THREATENING HIGHWAY AND
PEDESTRIAN SAFETY. MEASURES ARE NEEDED TO STOP OR REDUCE THROUGH
TRAFFIC.

3.   POLICY TR29 SHOULD BE STRENGTHENED TO STOP ALL DEVELOPMENT
ON WOODSIDE LANE UNTIL THE JUNCTION WITH THE MAIN ROAD IS
IMPROVED.
THE POLICY SHOULD NOT JUST 'CONSIDER' HIGHWAY IMPLICATIONS OF
DEVELOPMENT UNTIL THE JUNCTION IS IMPROVED. THE HIGHWAY AUTHORITY
ACKNOWLEDGES THE JUNCTION IS A SERIOUS ROAD HAZARD.

(If there is not enough room, please continue on a separate sheet)

Signature   *D Milton*   Date   31st MAY 2001

or a short letter of objection to a planning application. The reasons you give can be brief but must be clearly stated and on the relevant planning points so they let the council know what concerns you and what changes you want to see in the plan. You can expand on these reasons later. If you make a representation in support of a plan, to oppose someone else's objection, and you want to speak at the inquiry, say so now. Add a note at the bottom of the form.

Keep a copy of the completed form for your records. Be sure to send the required number of copies to the district council within the objection period - the full address is usually on the form or in the attached notes. Each separate objection is given a reference number by the council, which you'll be told. A copy of your objection form will be available for public inspection with all the other objections made.

If you don't want to do any more, just filling in the objection form can be the end of your active participation in the Local Plan. It isn't so daunting that your supporters should be put off registering their opposition too.

Local Plans attract varying numbers of objections: only 100 objections were made to Wansbeck District Local Plan, which is an unusually low number, while East Lindsay Local Plan in Lincolnshire attracted 2000 comments. Unless every objector is happy to put his case in writing, there'll be a Local Plan inquiry and it's very unusual for there not to be one. The district council appoints a programme officer who's employed by the council to administer objections and to liaise between the inspector, district council and objectors.

Some time after you send your Local Plan objection form, the planning officers contact you. If they think there's scope to negotiate over your objections a meeting will probably be arranged. If you reach agreement, the officers should put forward a modification to the plan. The inspector considers this modification together with all other suggested changes to the plan. Where you don't reach agreement, or only partially, press on with your objection. You can explain how far you have reached agreement in your statement or at the inquiry.

In any event, the council sends you another form to find out how you are going to back up your objection and whether you withdraw some or all of your objections. You have to say whether you want to rely on your objection form, add to the objection in writing or speak at the inquiry. If you intend taking part in the inquiry, record on the form whether you intend to deal with the objection personally, use a consultant or advocate, and whether you're going to have other expert witnesses (planning consultant, highway engineer, landscape architect or others). Return the completed form to the council by the date specified, taking a copy for your records. Unless you intend to rely on your objection form alone, you now need to think about preparing your case.

Objection statements

Whether you plan to attend the Local Plan inquiry or explain your reasons in writing, you need to draw up an objection statement - but not necessarily immediately. You should be told either by the programme officer or find out at a pre-inquiry meeting (see below) when statements should be submitted. A date is also set for the district council to produce its statement in response to your objection. If you want to speak at the inquiry, however, you don't have to submit a statement but it's usually better to say something in writing, even if it's brief, just in case.

Representations in favour of the plan and against other objections can be slightly more difficult than objections to the plan itself. Before you embark on writing a long and detailed statement, speak to the planning officers. Find out what they intend doing. There's no point in duplicating effort yet the district council can't be relied on to fight every objection. It might, on reflection, agree with some and argue for a modification to its own draft plan in line with the objection. It's the plan as published which is the starting point for the Local Plan inspector's consideration so make sure you know the council's reaction. If the council isn't going to make all the points you want made or the planning officer suggests it would be a good idea, write your own statement supporting the relevant plan policy. Regardless of whether you get the opportunity to see the other objector's case first, still send your statement to the council by the given date. Look at the objector's case afterwards and make comments on it in writing or at the inquiry. Bear in mind, though, that people supporting the plan don't have an automatic right to take part in the inquiry. Alternatively, the council could call you to give evidence as part of its case.

A Local Plan objection statement is similar to a letter of objection to a planning application or to written representations on a planning appeal, except that with applications and appeals you are reacting to aspects of a specific proposal (see Chapters 2 and 3). Local Plans deal with development at a more general level. Land allocated for development might be no more than a line drawn around the site on a proposals map. Policies set guidance for the sort of situations where certain types of development would be allowed. You must think about the implications of policies at this general level. Points such as overlooking neighbouring properties, design and site layout are seldom relevant to Local Plans.

There's no set length or form for a Local Plan objection statement. It could be a letter on two or three sides of A4 paper. Concise clear statements are the most effective, including any plans, drawings, photographs and illustrations that might be helpful to your case. Start your statement with an introduction, setting out what your objection relates to and mentioning if you represent a group or other individual objectors. Where you object to the plan because it doesn't include policies you feel it should, try to come up with a succinct statement of the policy you want to see put into the Local Plan.

Then go on to location and description. Where your objection is about a particular site, describe where it is, what it's like and the surrounding area. Where you object to a policy that applies to a wide area or throughout the district, describe the relevant characteristics: for example, where a policy affects development in an existing residential area, describe its character and the features you want to see preserved. The history and development of the town or district could be helpful to your case; if it has a bearing on the issues, put it in. In the background section of a statement you can deal with existing and past uses of a site and any previous planning decisions there are. Remember, planning applications and appeals might have been turned down on points of detail rather than underlying principle.

Include a section in your statement on planning policy if it's relevant as Local Plan policies should be consistent with each other, the county Structure Plan and general government planning policy. Although the county council itself looks at the Local Plan to check it generally conforms to the Structure Plan, there might still be points to draw from Structure Plan policies. In the issues and conclusions section draw all the information together to form a compelling case for what you propose. Say what changes should be made to improve the plan or what defects in it need correcting.

When your statement is finished, ask the programme officer how many copies to send. The council will pass one copy to the inspector and make one copy available for the public. Keep at least one copy for yourself. If you're not taking part in the Local Plan inquiry, that's all you need do until the Local Plan inspector's report is published months later. The council should contact you to let you know the result of your objection. There are steps you can take then and we deal with this later in this Chapter.

LOCAL PLAN INQUIRIES

Although objections and representations are made to the district council, it's the Local Plan inspector who considers these, either at a Local Plan inquiry, or in writing. His or her recommendations are very important, yet not binding on the district council. A Local Plan inquiry is very similar to a planning appeal inquiry (see Chapter 3). The main difference is that at a Local Plan inquiry numerous objections are discussed and consequently it can last many weeks or even months. It also tends to be less formal: objectors often take part without being represented by professionals. The system is supposed to allow full public participation, and inspectors and planning officers do their best to make it as easy for you as they can.

If you don't want to speak at the inquiry, that's fine - your written statement is taken into account by the inspector - or you can turn up at the inquiry as an observer. Taking part, however, does give you the opportunity to put questions to the council and to other objectors. Regardless of whether you're familiar with inquiries, it's worthwhile attending the pre-inquiry meeting and if you've made an objection, you'll be notified of the meeting in advance. You can pick up useful pointers to the character of the inspector and how he wants to deal with things. Comply with this as far as possible. The inspector will also say when statements should be submitted prior to an objection being discussed at the inquiry. It isn't, however, appropriate to go into the merits of individual cases at the pre-inquiry meeting. Don't worry if you can't make it to this meeting. The programme officer usually writes up notes from the meeting and you can get a copy. He then sends a timetable for the inquiry to all objectors. This shows when each objector is due to appear at the inquiry and how much time is allotted to discuss the objection. Contact the programme officer immediately if you can't attend at the time allocated to you. Where you make more than one objection, it's possible that you have to turn up at the inquiry more than once. Inquiry timetables are often arranged around main issues so that all discussion on a particular topic takes place only once.

If you definitely want to speak out against someone else's objection at the Local Plan inquiry, raise this at the pre-inquiry meeting, or let the programme officer know in advance. You also need to check when the objection in question is going to be discussed.

Presenting your objections

By the time you appear at the inquiry you should've submitted your arguments in writing. If the district council opposes your objection, you should've received its statement. Study this thoroughly, in the way recommended in Chapter 3. If there are points in the council's statement you don't understand, speak to the planning officer about them before you attend the inquiry. There might be things you need to check or further work to do. Remember to make notes ready for the questions.

At the Local Plan inquiry itself, the inspector will guide you through the process. If your own statement is short, you might be asked to read it out. Otherwise, you'll be asked to summarise your case. This is to set the scene, especially for any members of the public who are present; the inspector and the planning officer will have read your statement already. When you finish your introduction you'll be asked questions by the district council's advocate, usually a solicitor or barrister, and by the inspector. These can be about anything in your statement and about points made by the council. The council's advocate will then present the district council's case, and you and the inspector can question the planning officer direct about it. The council's advocate sums up the council's case in support of the plan as it is, or as the council has modified it.

Fortunately, you have the last word. Briefly re-state your best points and, if you can, mention anything helpful to your case that came out of the discussion at the inquiry. When you finish, the inspector will say that discussion about that objection is concluded. The inquiry moves on to the next objection.

Opposing other objections

When you want to oppose someone else's objection at the Local Plan inquiry, you should've already made a representation in support of the plan policy. You might also have sent a written statement to the council about the objection. This is given full weight by the inspector and by the council. Any support for the plan is supposed to be dealt with in this way and the inspector is not bound to let you speak at the inquiry. Inspectors, however, have discretion on this. Normally, you have to show that you want to raise issues that the council is not going to. This means you need to contact the planning officers to find out what they'll say and whether there's anything further you can add. When the objection is dealt with at the inquiry, unless you've got agreement about speaking in advance, there's likely to be some discussion over whether you can take part. Be ready to distinguish what you want to say from what the council says.

The district council can agree with the objection, entirely or in part, or oppose it. Its statement, which you might not be sent automatically, should make its stance clear. Contact the planning officer beforehand if you are in any doubt.

Objectors might be represented by a barrister and professional witnesses. They present their case first, the council will ask questions and you put yours. The council will then present its case: thereafter questions can be put to them by objectors or by their representatives. You then have your say: give your own particular reasons for supporting the plan as it stands and explain the disadvantages of the objectors' alternative. After the objectors have questioned you, the council will sum up its case. The objectors have the last word and the inspector closes discussion on that objection.

INSPECTORS' SITE VISITS

Local Plan site inspections can take place immediately after an objection has been heard, after all the objections have been heard, which might be weeks after you discussed your objection, or at other times during the inquiry. Objectors who take part in the inquiry normally attend the site visit which is arranged by the programme officer - but not during your formal appearance at the inquiry itself. He'll contact you to arrange a date and time. You can't discuss the merits of a case at a Local Plan site visit.

THE DECISION

When all objections have been heard at the inquiry and site inspections made, the Local Plan inspector considers each case and reports his recommendations to the council (see Figure 5.6).

Inspector's report

The report, which can take anything between a few months and a year to write, sets out the inspector's findings on all objections. For each objection, or group of objections, there's a summary of the objector's case and the council's response. The inspector says what conclusion he's reached and whether he agrees with the plan as it is or whether he recommends changes. Planning officers go through the report, and draw up draft modifications. These are put to a planning committee for approval. This is another opportunity to speak to councillors and lobby for the changes you want as the council doesn't have to follow the inspector's recommendations - although in most cases it will. Whether or not the council follows an inspector's suggested changes to the plan, his opinions and comments on a site or issue might still be influential if a subsequent planning application is made.

The council should tell you whether it intends to change the plan in the light of your objection and the inspector's report. It might send you the relevant part of the inspector's report. If it doesn't, go to the planning department and ask to see it. The inspector's report and list of proposed modifications, together with reasons for them, is available for public inspection. Read what the inspector said, what his conclusions are and whether he recommends any changes. See how the council's proposed changes, or lack of them, compare.

CHALLENGING DECISIONS

During the six-week period for objecting to modifications proposed by the council, you can object to a proposed modification as well as to the council's failure to modify, where the inspector's report recommends that it should. You can't, however, object to the original plan again. Make your objection on the form the planning department provides, following the guidelines about making objections and representations as previously described. Sometimes another inquiry is held into objections to modifications. This

---

FIGURE 5.6 A Typical Inspector's Report on an Objection Following a Local Plan Inquiry

Introduction
This objection concerns the Local Plan provision and policies concerning open space within a largely urban Borough.

Commentary
4.67 I support the council's proposed changes to the open space policies which now appear to meet the objections to a great extent. The effect of the wildlife strategy has been considered and I believe the changed policies and supporting text agree with the council's aim to provide the best possible environment for residents without imposing strict restraints on the development needed to keep the town alive. Loss of public open space should be matched by new provision of at least equal standard. I understand the desire to protect private playing fields but the best use for each site should be a matter for detailed consideration when an application for development is made.

Recommendations
R312   page 72, Policy ENV35: delete the policy and replace with:
"PLANNING PERMISSION FOR THE DEVELOPMENT OF EXISTING PUBLIC OPEN SPACE WILL BE REFUSED UNLESS IT IS TO PROVIDE PUBLIC OR COMMUNITY RECREATIONAL FACILITIES FOR DEMONSTRATED NEEDS OR UNLESS EQUALLY VALUABLE REPLACEMENT PROVISION IS MADE UNDER PROPOSALS IN THIS PLAN. THE IMPACT OF SUCH FACILITIES ON THE TOWNSCAPE, LANDSCAPE AND LOCAL COMMUNITY WILL BE CAREFULLY ASSESSED."

R313   page 73, Policy ENV36: delete the policy and replace with:
"OPPORTUNITIES FOR CREATING FURTHER AMENITY SPACE AND NATURAL HABITATS WILL BE TAKEN THROUGH ENVIRONMENTAL IMPROVEMENT SCHEMES AND LANDSCAPING SCHEMES REQUIRED FOR NEW DEVELOPMENTS."

happens when objections raise issues that weren't considered previously, where the council puts forward new policies or where modifications made to meet objections are subsequently withdrawn. In most cases further inquiries don't take place.

If the council goes against an inspector's recommendation in your favour, or you think the plan does not follow government policy, you can write to the DTLR, Northern Irish Planning Service, Scottish Executive or Welsh Assembly urging the government to direct the council to modify the Local Plan in some way. In more extreme cases, the government can call-in the whole Local Plan in the same way that planning applications can be called-in. Call-in powers are used when:

- the Local Plan doesn't appear to conform with national or regional policies or with the county Structure Plan
- where it raises important issues on a national or regional scale
- where it's very controversial, possibly affecting other areas
- where there are outstanding objections from the Department of the Environment, Food and Rural Affairs

South Cambridgeshire District Council, for example, was directed to change a policy putting restrictions on employment in a business park as this was contrary to government policy.

After objections to modifications have been dealt with, with or without an inquiry, councillors vote to adopt the Local Plan. This formal procedural step marks completion of the preparation of a Local Plan. If you're still unhappy, Local Plans, like planning appeal decisions, can be challenged in the courts on limited grounds. Procedural complaints can also be investigated (see Chapter 2).

LOCAL PLANS - ACTION CHECK LIST

1 Find out from the council when a Local Plan is being prepared.

2 Check the dates for making comments and objections.

3 Study the plan and make notes.

4 Discuss your concerns and queries with a planning officer and stay in touch to monitor progress.

5 Lobby councillors and consultees.

6 Alert other potential objectors and the media.

7 Write a letter to the council at the consultation stage.

8 Complete and send an objection form to the council during the deposit period.

9 Draw up a statement in support of your objection and send it to the council.

10 Prepare for and attend the Local Plan inquiry.

11 Read the Local Plan inspector's report and the council's statement and proposed modifications. Contact planning officers and councillors again.

12 Check the final result of your objection with the council.

Some areas and buildings are subject to special designations for planning purposes and we now look more closely at the most common ones: Tree Preservation Orders, Green Belts, National Parks, Areas of Outstanding Natural Beauty/National Scenic Areas, Sites of Special Scientific Interest, Conservation Areas, Listed Buildings, archaeological sites and those under 'article 4' directions. Such special cases not only attract additional planning restrictions in themselves but also receive more protection from development proposals that might jeopardise their special qualities.

The special designations, or cases, described in this chapter have their basis in planning law. There are others that you might come across in a Local Plan and councils' planning policy documents that don't have the same legal status as they're informal designations created by the council itself (see Chapter 1).

TREE PRESERVATION ORDERS

Tree Preservation Orders (TPOs) are made to protect trees that have amenity value, that is, they make a valuable contribution to the surrounding area, and can be put on single trees, small groups, areas or woodlands. Planning law doesn't, however, define 'tree' for TPO purposes which can cause problems where, for example, a TPO applies to an area of woodland, individual trees aren't specified. What sizes and species are covered is debatable. It's generally said that, for TPO purposes, the word 'tree' should have its ordinary meaning: a perennial plant with a woody trunk and branches. TPOs, therefore, don't include bushes and shrubs. The order shows the position of the trees on a map and states the species (see Figure 6.1). Single trees and trees within groups are specified individually. Trees in Conservation Areas automatically have similar protection to TPO trees (see pages 119).

With a few exceptions, a TPO tree shouldn't be cut down, topped, lopped, uprooted or damaged without the consent of the district council, which makes TPOs and keeps records of them. Applications to carry out work on TPO trees are like planning applications: applicants identify the trees, say what work they want to do and give reasons for the work. These applications, however, don't have to be advertised. You can object to TPO applications in the same way as you would a planning application (see Chapter 2). Remember, however, that trees aren't permanent: they have a natural life span and need occasional work to keep them healthy and safe.

A council can refuse an application to carry out work to a TPO tree or grant consent with conditions, such as the requirement to replant. An applicant can appeal to the Secretary of State for the Environment, Transport and the Regions, Northern Ireland Planning Appeals Commission, Scottish Executive, or Welsh Assembly. Shrewsbury and Atcham Borough Council, for example, refused permission to fell a 5.5 metre (18 foot) high protected oak tree stump that had all its branches removed under a previous permission. The owner argued it didn't have any amenity value but the council said it would grow again. The owner's appeal was dismissed.

In theory, TPOs are made to protect important trees, but in practice councils use them to help stop development or for greater control over it. Developers, for example, often prefer to deal with clear sites. Their first job, sometimes before making a planning application, is to send in the bulldozers to remove every living thing from a site. Pre-emptive TPOs can stop this: before selling off six cemeteries, Edinburgh District Council made TPOs covering all of the 2,000 trees in five of them, the remaining cemetery being protected by an order already.

If work on TPO trees or other valuable trees is taking place and concerns you, telephone the landscape officer in the planning department to see whether permission is needed or has been given. He or she might be able to take immediate action.

GREEN BELTS

Green Belts are formally designated areas of land drawn around certain cities; the term 'Green Belt' doesn't mean any open countryside or the land surrounding every town, as is frequently believed. Only land that's to be kept permanently open should be included in the Green Belt. The purposes of Green Belts are to stop urban sprawl, safeguard surrounding countryside, prevent towns merging, preserve special character of historic towns and help urban regeneration. About 12 per cent of England is included in Green Belts; that around London alone covers 486,000 hectares (1,200,000 acres) (see Figure 6.2). Green Belts are defined in development plans - their broad location in county

FIGURE 6.1 Typical Tree Preservation Order

SCHEDULE

No. on map   Description   Situation

Trees specified individually *(encircled in black on the map)*

    T.1   1 Oak   Land adj Leaf Lane, Branchley

    T.2   1 Ash   As above

Trees specified by reference to an Area *(within a dotted black line on the map)*

    A.1   Area consisting of scattered   As above
                specimens of Ash,
                Common Alder

Groups of trees *(within a broken black line on the map)*

    G.1   6 Ash   Land adj North Lane, Branchley

Woodlands *(within a continuous black line on the map)*

    W.1   Mixed deciduous woodland: Land adj Leaf Lane, Branchley
                comprising Oak, Ash,
                Hornbeam, Cherry

Structure Plans and the detail of precise boundaries (usually features such as roads, streams and tree belts) in Local Plans. Therefore, if you want to have a say in what land is or isn't included in a Green Belt, get involved in the preparation of the relevant Local Plan (see Chapter 5). Land allocated as part of the Green Belt is unlikely to be built on and, once established, the boundaries aren't supposed to be changed.

Green Belts are controlled by strict planning policies that prevent all but a few limited types of development. They're one place where there's a general presumption against development taking place. Except in very special circumstances, planning permission shouldn't be given other than for agriculture and forestry, outdoor sports, cemeteries, limited infilling in developed areas and re-use of existing buildings. Mining and quarrying can be allowed where suitable environmental protection and restoration of the land is ensured. This doesn't, however, stop councils trying to release Green Belt land for development. For example, in drawing up its Unitary Development Plan, the City of Leeds proposed allocating a site in the Green Belt for a business park and 1,000 houses.

Where you're concerned with individual development proposals, inappropriate development in the Green Belt is a very powerful argument to use. Think how the proposal would affect the purposes of the Green Belt, and look in the Local Plan to see what the specific Green Belt policies are.

NATIONAL PARKS

National Parks are specially protected areas of attractive countryside in which the public are encouraged to seek enjoyment. Some 10 per cent of England and Wales is designated National Park, and the Norfolk and Suffolk broads and the New Forest, although not actually so designated, have the same status (see Figure 6.3). There are no National Parks as yet in Scotland or Northern Ireland but there are proposals for more designations in various locations throughout the UK. National Parks are designated by the Countryside Agency, Scottish Natural Heritage and Countryside Council for Wales, with the approval of government. National Parks have their own authorities, which deal with planning matters

---

FIGURE 6.2 Green Belts in the United Kingdom

England
- Avon
- Burton-Swadlincote
- Cambridge
- Gloucester, Cheltenham
- Greater Manchester, Central Lancashire
- Lancaster and Flyde Coast
- London

- Merseyside, Wirral
- Nottingham, Derby
- Oxford
- South West Hampshire/South East Dorset
- South and West Yorkshire
- Stoke-on-Trent
- Tyne & Wear
- West Midlands

- York

Scotland
- Aberdeen
- Ayr/Prestwick
- Edinburgh
- Falkirk/Grangemouth
- Greater Glasgow

Northern Ireland
- Belfast

---

and are like district councils. They draw up Structure and Local Plans covering the whole of the National Park and decide planning applications in their area.

Inside National Parks, the types of development for which planning permission is automatically granted are more restricted (see Chapter 1). There are thus no 'permitted development' rights for roof extensions, cladding the outside of houses, satellite dishes on chimneys, tall buildings and facing roads and for excavations for fish farming. There are also lower limits for extensions to houses and industrial buildings and for buildings in the grounds of houses. Siting and design of extensions and alterations to agricultural buildings under the 'permitted development' regime can be controlled by National Park authorities. Look out for Local Plans being prepared for National Parks. See what's proposed and make your views on development in the park known during that process. Local Plans for National Parks concentrate largely on conserving natural beauty but must also take into account the prosperity and social well being of the area.

The same factors come into play when planning applications are submitted. Apart from looking at the effect on scenery, proposals are expected to reflect traditional local styles of building and materials. The conversion of a stone building to a game keeper's cottage, for example, was not allowed in Brecon Beacons National Park. The site was in attractive open countryside close to a public footpath and conversion wouldn't retain the character of the building. The game keeper's duties were geared to sporting shoots, not strictly agriculture, and were only seasonal.

Large scale development including mining and quarrying should only take place in National Parks in exceptional circumstances and applicants must prove such development is in the public interest. Three criteria apply:

- the need for the development nationally and locally
- the opportunities for locating it somewhere outside the National Park or meeting the needs in a different way
- the degree of harm to the environment and landscape and how that could be minimised

So, for example, British Nuclear Fuels was given planning permission to drill test bore holes in the Lake District National Park as the survey information needed in connection with nearby Sellafield couldn't be collected in any other way.

Where you're concerned with development in National Parks, the designation gives further scope for your objection. Because National Parks are designated in recognition of the national importance of their landscape, you should develop your argument along those lines. Assess the impact the proposal would have on the scenery and see how the proposed development would fit in with the existing buildings. The Countryside Agency and Countryside Council for Wales produce advice for development in National Parks so contact them to find out whether they have published anything relevant to your case (see Appendix II).

FIGURE 6.3 National Parks, Areas of Outstanding Natural Beauty and National Scenic Areas in the United Kingdom

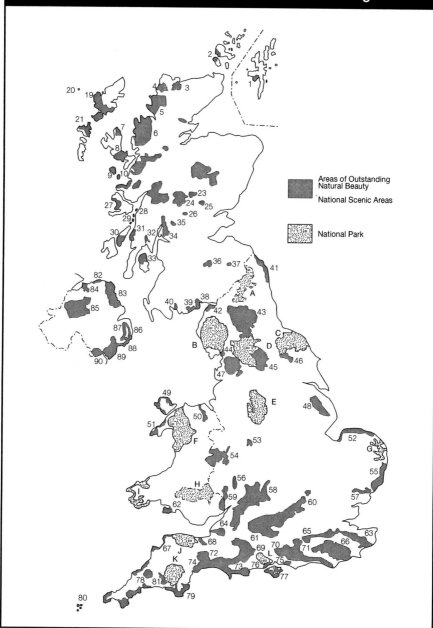

NATIONAL PARKS (ENGLAND AND WALES)

A	Northumberland	G	The Broads
B	Lake District	H	Brecon Beacons
C	North York Moors	I	Pembrokeshire Coast
D	Yorkshire Dales	J	Exmoor
E	Peak District	K	Dartmoor
F	Snowdonia	L	New Forest Heritage Area

NATIONAL SCENIC AREAS (SCOTLAND)

1	Shetland	21	South Uist Machair
2	Hoy and West Mainland	22	Deeside and Lochnagar
3	Kyle of Tongue	23	Loch Tummel
4	N. W. Sutherland	24	Lock Rannock and Glen Lyon
5	Assynt-Coigach	25	River Tay (Dunkeld)
6	Wester Ross	26	River Earn (Comrie to St Fillans)
7	Trotternish	27	Loch na Keal, Isle of Mull
8	The Cullin Hills	28	Lynn of Lorn
9	The Small Isles	29	Scarba, Lunga and the Garvellachs
10	Morar, Moidart and Ardnamurchan	30	Jura
11	Loch Shiel	31	Knapdale
12	Knoydart	32	Kyles of Bute
13	Kintail	33	North Arran
14	Glen Affric	34	Lock Lomond
15	Glen Strathfarrar	35	The Trossachs
16	Dornoch Firth	36	Upper Tweedale
17	Ben Nevis and Glen Coe	37	Eildon and Leaderfoot
18	The Cairngorm Mountains	38	Nith Estuary
19	South Lewis, Harris and North Uist	39	East Stewarty Coast
20	St Kilda	40	Fleet Valley

AREAS OF OUTSTANDING NATURAL BEAUTY

Like National Parks, Areas of Outstanding Natural Beauty (AONBs) are specially protected areas of countryside of national importance. The equivalent designation in Scotland is the National Scenic Area (NSA). In AONBs the needs of agriculture and other rural businesses and those of local communities still have to be taken into account even though the primary purpose of AONBs is to conserve and enhance natural beauty.

FIGURE 6.3 National Parks, Areas of Outstanding Natural Beauty and National Scenic Areas in the United Kingdom Cont...

AREAS OF OUTSTANDING NATURAL BEAUTY (ENGLAND, WALES AND NORTHERN IRELAND)

England and Wales

41 Northumberland Coast
42 Solway Coast
43 North Pennines
44 Arnside and Silverdale
45 Nidderdale
46 Howardian Hills
47 Forest of Bowland
48 Lincolnshire Wolds
49 Anglesey
50 Clwydian Range
51 Llyen
52 Norfolk Coast
53 Cannock Chase
54 Shropshire Hills
55 Suffolk Coasts and Heaths
56 Malvern Hills
57 Dedham Vale
58 Cotswolds
59 Wye Valley
60 Chilterns
61 North Wessex Downs
62 Gower
63 Kent Downs
64 Mendip Hills
65 Surrey Hills
66 High Weald

67 North Devon
68 Quantock Hills
69 Cranborne Chase and West Wiltshire Downs
70 East Hampshire
71 Sussex Downs
72 Blackdown Hills
73 Dorset
74 East Devon
75 Chichester Harbour
76 South Hampshire Coast
77 Isle of Wight
78 Cornwall
79 South Devon
80 Isles of Scilly
81 Tamar Valley

Northern Ireland

82 Causeway Coast
83 Antrim Coast and Glen
84 North Derry
85 Sperrin
86 Strangford Lough
87 Langan Valley
88 Lecale Coast
89 Mourne
90 Ring of Gullion

Unlike National Parks, public access isn't an objective of AONBs; recreation is encouraged but only if it's compatible with conservation of natural beauty. Around 90 AONBs and NSAs have been designated covering about one sixth of the land area of the United Kingdom (see Figure 6.3).

County Structure Plans indicate the general location of an AONB and proposals maps in Local Plans show the boundaries. District councils also have even more detailed maps where you can check boundaries more precisely than in the Local Plan. AONB boundaries aren't set through the Local Plan process. You can't, therefore, get land near the edge of existing AONBs included through involvement in the Local Plan, nor can the district council itself designate new areas. You can, however, try to influence the Local Plan policies that apply in AONBs.

There are no special planning authorities for AONBs. Structure and Local Plans and the control of development are carried out by the county and district councils for the area, so that AONBs are covered by different planning authorities with slightly different planning policies. In addition to Structure and Local Plans, county and district councils often draw up informal policy documents for AONBs. These describe the features and character that make the area special and that need to be protected and set out the pressures on the area and what the councils plan to do to enhance the AONB.

The limits on 'permitted development' rights in National Parks also apply in AONBs (see page 9). Development allowed in AONBs is generally small-scale, associated with the existing villages and properties or related to agriculture. The design and materials of new buildings are supposed to reflect local architecture and be situated unobtrusively, yet, in a controversial decision, the Secretary of State permitted a Centre Parcs holiday village in the AONB at Longleat, Wiltshire. The Council for the Protection of Rural England and Lovers of Longleat Association opposed it at the public inquiry but planning permission was granted because the development was an employment generating tourism proposal, which was in the national interest. It would be contained within existing woods and involve further large scale tree planting.

If a planning application that concerns you falls within an AONB, the designation will probably be an important factor in the decision. Find out what features of the landscape are recognised in planning policies and use your own judgement. Assess particularly the effect on these features and the impact on views of the landscape.

SITES OF SPECIAL SCIENTIFIC INTEREST

Sites of Special Scientific Interest (SSSIs) are areas designated to protect their wildlife or geological features. There are over 5,500 SSSIs in the United Kingdom covering roughly 8% of the country. About 70% of these are designated because of their wildlife value, about 20% because of their geology, and the remaining ones for both reasons. In addition to SSSI status, some areas have extra designations (see Figure 6.4).

It's a criminal offence to carry out some activities in SSSIs without consent so owners and occupiers of these sites must notify English Nature, or the equivalent Scottish, Welsh and Northern Irish bodies, if they want to carry out activities prohibited in the original SSSI notification. If you fear something is being done in or near an SSSI which is causing damage, get in touch with the district council immediately. The officers can investigate and tell you whether the activity is allowed or take action to stop it. In an emergency, say at the weekend, you could contact the police.

FIGURE 6.4 Additional Nature Conservation Designations that apply to some Sites of Special Scientific Interest

Ramsar Site	internationally important wetlands and habitat of waterfowl
Special Protection Area	habitat of threatened bird species, part of European-wide 'Natura 2000' network of sites
Special Area of Conservation	habitat of endangered species, part of European-wide 'Natura 2000' network of sites
National Nature Reserve	area of national or international importance controlled by English Nature, Scottish Natural Heritage or Countryside Council for Wales and used primarily for nature conservation
Biogenetic Reserve	area for conservation of heathland and dry grassland
Marine Nature Reserve	equivalent in status to SSSI applying to areas covered by tidal waters or sea for conservation of marine wildlife and geology

Some 'permitted development' rights such as holding war games, motor sports and clay pigeon shoots are automatically restricted in SSSIs. District councils can also make formal directions which take away other 'permitted development' rights that might harm an SSSI. If you think development proposals might affect an SSSI, check the Local Plan or ask about the site at the planning department. You can also ask to see the notification which shows the location and extent of the designated site, and what its special features are. Note the features and the relevant planning policies and use these in your objections. Development isn't banned completely but it's unusual for planning permission to be granted actually in SSSIs and it's more often the effect on nearby SSSIs that's the issue.

When a planning application is made for any development in an SSSI or for development outside but which might still affect it, either English Nature, the Environment Service of the Northern Ireland DoE, Scottish Natural Heritage or the Countryside Council for Wales is consulted. Consultation areas are defined around SSSIs for this purpose. If a council decides to grant planning permission, against the advice of one of these conservation bodies, the latter can ask the government to call in the application (see Chapter 2).

If a site or land that has some wildlife or geological interest is under threat of development, try to have it protected. Contact the local Wildlife Trust; the district council or your local library should have the address, if it's not in the telephone book. Alternatively, contact the officer who deals with nature conservation at the district council. He or she might be able to assist because district councils can establish Local Nature Reserves and make bylaws. Local Nature Reserves are not SSSIs but locally important wildlife habitats and their purpose is to conserve nature and provide the opportunity for the public to see wildlife. You could also contact English Nature or equivalent body (see Appendix II) which will probably refer you to one of its regional offices.

CONSERVATION AREAS

Conservation Areas are parts of towns and villages designated for their architectural or historic value (see Figure 6.5). There are over 9,000 Conservation Areas and new ones are designated every year. Most large towns have at least one Conservation Area and all districts will have some: Cotswold District, Gloucestershire, has more than 140.

Conservation Areas vary widely in size. Some cover whole town centres, others cover squares or small groups of buildings. The features that justify the designation are also varied - buildings dating from the same period or of a uniform style, medieval street patterns, areas around village greens and parks - but each area must possess its own special character. Listed Buildings often form the core of Conservation Areas (see page 121).

Such areas have tighter planning controls than areas not so designated. Permission, called Conservation Area consent, is needed to demolish most buildings and structures. An application, like a planning application, is made to the council, usually at the same time as planning permission is applied for. Planning applications for development that would affect the character or appearance of a Conservation Area must be advertised in a local newspaper and site notices put up.

Any proposed felling or other work on trees in Conservation Areas has to be notified to the council. If the council doesn't want the work to take place, it makes a Tree Preservation Order to prevent it (see page 109). Demolition of buildings and work on trees without permission or notification in Conservation Areas is a criminal offence so, if you're concerned by buildings being demolished or trees being felled, check with the planning department whether consent has been given. In an emergency, you could try contacting the police to stop unauthorised work being carried out.

The types of development for which planning permission is automatically granted are restricted in Conservation Areas. There are thus limits on 'permitted development' rights for:

• house and roof extensions
• cladding the outside of houses
• the size of outbuildings
• satellite dishes on chimneys, tall buildings or facing roads
• the size of extensions to industrial buildings
• some telecommunications equipment

FIGURE 6.5 Typical Conservation Areas

Kempston Conservation Area, Bedford, Bedfordshire

Kempston is in the outskirts of Bedford. The Conservation Area is based on High Street and Water Lane, which retains a village character. Most Listed Buildings at Kempston are in the Conservation Area.

Many buildings are Victorian. Some date from seventeenth century. Pink bricks from local brickworks characterise the area. Water Lane is narrow with buildings of different styles set at varying angles to the road, reflecting its organic development.

High Street has a variety of architecture, including the half-timbered black-and-white King William pub and a group of old stone buildings.

A small copse of mixed deciduous trees at the end of High Street complements the older properties and is a positive feature in the street.

Brunswick Town Conservation Area, Hove, East Sussex

The Conservation Area is based around a number of squares on the seafront. It includes 500 Listed Buildings, more than 100 are Grade I.

Brunswick Square and Brunswick Terrace date from 1820's with designs by Wilde and Busby. The Brunswick Estate was extended in the early Victorian period. Adelaide Crescent, originally designed by Decimus Burton, was completed with the adjoining Palmeira Square 1850-60 by Sir Isaac Lyon Goldsmid.

The Conservation Area exhibits one of the finest examples of Regency and early Victorian architecture and planned estates.

Long Preston Conservation Area, Yorkshire Dales National Park

Long Preston is a village that sits astride the A65 on the edge of the National Park. An important element of the character is the historic network of lanes, which lead to pastures above the village.

The Conservation Area incorporates several outlying groups of buildings that form part of the extended village setting. The area covers twenty-five Listed Buildings, including a fourteenth century Grade I listed church. Also in the area is a scheduled Roman fort and four other sites with known archaeological interest.

Councils can take away other automatic 'permitted development' rights, but only where the particular character of Conservation Areas is threatened by types of development that can go ahead without a planning application (see Chapter 1).

Development proposals in Conservation Areas are looked at very closely by councils to make sure they fit in with the established character. This doesn't mean development isn't allowed, but more emphasis is put on things such as design, building materials and appearance. District councils usually insist on full details of proposals rather than deciding outline planning applications. This applies to most sites where 'reserved matters' - siting, design, layout, access, landscaping - are all important. The careful scrutiny of planning applications can apply to properties near to Conservation Areas. Proposals outside can still affect the character of the formally designated area. For example, Gloucestershire County Council's proposals for the design and layout of new magistrates courts in the centre of Gloucester were dismissed at appeal, although outline planning permission had already been given. The site was near a Conservation Area and the inspector felt that the design was at odds with the area when looked at as a whole, even though it was acceptable when looked at in isolation.

When you react to planning applications or appeals for development in Conservation Areas, look up the Local Plan policies. The supporting text often gives a description of the characteristics of the area. Ask at the planning department to see any report or consultation documents drawn up when the Conservation Area was designated. Sometimes the information can be sparse; in other cases, the documents provide a thorough description of the area and identify its important features. Use this to help make your arguments informed, precise and relevant. Check your Local Plan to find out whether planning policies give adequate protection to what you believe is important in Conservation Areas. Use the Local Plan process to get additional policies, more specific policies or firmer policies included (see Chapter 5).

LISTED BUILDINGS

Selected buildings and structures are given additional protection beyond normal planning control, because of their special architectural or historic value. Such Listed Buildings are entered on lists kept theoretically by the Secretary of State for Culture, Media and Sport, Northern Ireland Department of the Environment, Scottish Executive and Welsh Assembly. More than half a million buildings and structures are listed. They include not only complete buildings but also old-style telephone boxes, medieval walls, train sheds, water troughs, lamp posts and grave stones amongst other structures. Not only is the fabric of the Listed Building covered but also its internal features, including fixtures and fittings, any other buildings or structures fixed to the building (extensions, coach houses, railings) and anything in the grounds of the building (walls, fences, outbuildings).

Buildings are listed after appraisal and investigation by officers of English Heritage, Protecting Historic Buildings Branch of the Northern Ireland Environment and Heritage

FIGURE 6.6 Typical Listed Buildings Descriptions in the Statutory List

Country cottage

Late medieval, timber-framed; altered in C17 and more recently. Of two storeys and three bays; formerly having two bay hall to west, but this now floored across. Lower storey of C18 red brick except at west end where original framing survives. Hipped tiled roof; modern casements.

Hotel

Hotel, two builds, north part late C18, south part late C19 and not of special interest. North part painted brick with hipped tile roof. 2 storey, 3 windows, 16 pane sashes in moulded architraves to first floor, 2 tripartite sashes with horns to ground floor. Simple cambered doorcase. Late C18 scrolled wrought iron inn sign fixture. Brick chimney stack to rear. Interior contains heterogeneous collection of architectural salvage.

Town house

House. Early C19, red brick, the south front tile hung on first floor, with tiled roof. 2 storeys, 2 windows. Casement windows with wooden architraves and leaded lights to 1st floor. Ground floor has a right side tripartite casement and left side early C19 bow with 24 panes and reeded surrounds. Off central doorcase having door with cambered head and plank door.

Service, Historic Scotland, the Welsh Historic Monuments Executive Agency (CADW) - the government's advisory bodies on architecture and building conservation.

In emergencies, for example where demolition is threatened, buildings can be spot listed. This is a one-off decision rather than listing as part of wider survey of an area. In similar emergency circumstances, councils can serve a Building Preservation Notice, which provides Listed Building protection for six months. During that time the respective government advisory body decides whether to recommend listing the building permanently.

Three categories of listing distinguish the importance buildings, which in England and Wales are:

- Grade I, the most exceptional buildings; comprises only 2% of all Listed Buildings
- Grade II*, particularly important buildings; comprises about 4% of all Listed Buildings
- Grade II, buildings of special interest; comprises some 94% of all Listed Buildings

---

In Scotland, Listed Buildings are defined as:

- Category A, nationally important; comprises about 7% of all Scottish Listed Buildings
- Category B, locally important; comprises about 62% of all Scottish Listed Buildings
- Category Cs, good buildings with some element of interest; comprises about 31% of all Scottish Listed Buildings

There are no separate grades of Listed Buildings in Northern Ireland.

District councils keep a note of Listed Buildings in their areas, which you can inspect. The list sets out the address of each building and a short description for identification (see Figure 6.6). The description might be detailed but doesn't necessarily define all the important features nor the full extent of what is covered by the listing. This information is not actually given anywhere: planning officers, councillors, planning inspectors, and members of the public are left to decide for themselves what special features warrant protection.

Once a building is listed, all work which would affect its special character must have Listed Building consent. Work can be anything from demolition to minor alterations and painting, and it's a criminal offence to carry out unauthorised work. Listed Building applications and consents are like planning applications and planning permission. Additionally, planning applications which affect the setting of a Listed Building must be advertised in local papers and a notice is put up on the site (see Chapter 2). There's also a parallel system of Listed Building enforcement to stop and remedy unauthorised work. Applicants can appeal against refusal of Listed Building consent or enforcement.

Both Listed Building applications and planning applications that affect a Listed Building or its setting are subject to particularly close scrutiny. Extra weight is put on preserving the building, its setting and its features. Demolition isn't allowed unless every effort has been made to find a suitable use and, usually, the building should have been put up for sale first. All Listed Building proposals are assessed bearing in mind:

- the importance of the building, its rarity, and the contribution it makes to the area
- historical interest
- how well it illustrates past construction techniques
- the state of repair
- maintenance costs
- whether alternative uses would bring new life to or secure the future of the building

Decisions on development proposals on or near Listed Buildings turn largely on architectural merits. You can make your own judgements about questions of design but architecture might be an area in which you need help. Aside from getting professional advice (see Appendix I), contact local architectural associations or groups involved in preserving and restoring old buildings as they might support your objections. Some district councils have officers who deal specifically with architectural matters, often called 'conservation officers'. Others use architectural advisers from the country council. Find out who advises the planning officers and contact him to discuss a proposal.

A proposal for eighteen apartment units at the Abbey House Hotel, a Grade II* Listed Building at Barrow-in-Furness, Cumbria was turned down because the layout of historic parkland would have been compromised and urban characteristics introduced into the rural setting of the Listed Building. Similarly, a shop in Henley, Oxfordshire was prevented from putting up canopy blinds on the Grade II Listed Building: the blinds covered up important architectural details and spoiled the simple street elevation of the building.

If you feel an unlisted building or structure, possibly under threat from a planning proposal, is worthy of listing you can make a request for this to be done through the district council or local historical or architectural society, if it's prepared to take it up for you. Otherwise, you can make the request yourself (addresses to write to are in Appendix II). Westminster City Council planned to demolish the Millicent Fawcett Hall, associated with the suffragette movement, for re-development. Campaigners tried unsuccessfully three times to get it listed, but they succeeded eventually. The building was spot listed and was saved from demolition.

ARCHAEOLOGY

Of the 600,000 recorded archaeological sites in the United Kingdom, some 13,000 have, over the last 100 years, been designated Scheduled Ancient Monuments, which gives them special protection beyond the normal planning controls. The term 'Monuments' here covers buildings and structures above or below ground as well as sites with traces of previous existence, and remains of vehicles and vessels.

Scheduled Monuments rank alongside Grade I and Grade II* listed buildings in importance and their scheduling is very similar to the listing of a Listed Building (see page 121). The Secretary of State for Culture, Media and Sport, Northern Ireland Department of the Environment, Scottish Executive and Welsh Assembly maintain a schedule of ancient monuments which are nationally important. Full details of all known archaeological sites, including Scheduled Ancient Monuments, are recorded in Sites and Monuments Records (see Figure 6.7) by county councils, who have officers dealing with archaeology and advising district councils, or by unitary councils. Such a record for London is kept by English Heritage. In Northern Ireland contact Protection of Historic Monuments Branch of the Environment and Heritage Service.

Once scheduled, Scheduled Ancient Monument consent must be granted for any work involving demolition, damage, removal, alteration, repair or covering up the monument. Some kinds of work, however, are allowed automatically, rather like 'permitted development' (see Chapter 1). Applications for Scheduled Monument consent are made direct to the government. Applicants can ask for a hearing or the government can decide to hold a public inquiry but most applications are for minor works and so no hearing or inquiry is usually held. There's no formal public consultation procedure. If a development proposal involves a Scheduled Monument application and a planning application, any public inquiries will normally take place together.

If planning applications are made in areas where there might be archaeological interest, look up the Sites and Monuments Record map at the county council offices or its equivalent. The fact that a recorded site is affected isn't necessarily a reason for opposing development. Discuss the proposal with the archaeology officer and frame your arguments in the light of this discussion. Consider getting specialist advice if archaeology is going to be the main issue (see Appendix I). It's a criminal offence to carry out unauthorised work on a Scheduled Monument. Despite warnings from the police who were alerted by neighbours, a businessman knocked the top off a brick-and-flint wall in the grounds of a scheduled thirteenth-century castle at Bungay, Suffolk. For this he was fined £3,000.

Areas in which important remains are likely to be found are designated Areas of Archaeological Importance (AAIs). The historic town centres of Canterbury, Chester, Exeter, Hereford and York have so far been designated. Within such areas, six weeks notice has to be given to the district council of any proposals to disturb the ground, tip on it or flood it. The site can be investigated and the proposed development held up, if necessary, where excavation is needed.

Where development proposals affect sites that might have important archaeological remains, district councils can ask applicants to carry out field evaluations. This isn't a full excavation but an initial appraisal by a qualified archaeologist. If development affects archaeological remains, a balance needs to be struck between the merits of the development and the importance and nature of the remains. Applicants and district councils can agree for sites to be excavated before the development is carried out and district councils can include conditions that sites are excavated.

ARTICLE 4 DIRECTIONS

Article 4 directions limit the types of building work and changes of use that are generally allowed under the 'permitted development' rules which provide for a wide range of minor development to go ahead without a planning application (see Chapter 1). Where such minor development could be damaging, a district council can make an article 4 direction, which compels the owner to apply for planning permission. Most article 4 directions concern development in Conservation Areas and in attractive areas of countryside (see Figure 6.8). For example, a direction taking away temporary use rights

FIGURE 6.7 Typical Sites and Monuments Record Map

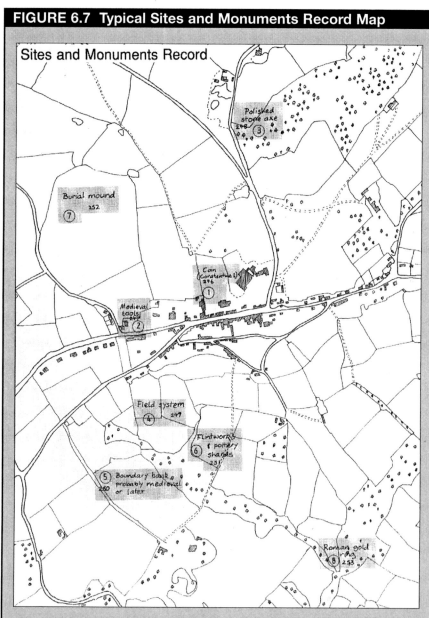

Sites and Monuments Record

Polished stone axe 248 ③

Burial mound 252 ⑦

Coin (Constantine I) 246 ①

Medieval tools 247 ②

Field system 249 ④

Flintwork & pottery shards 251 ⑥

Boundary bank probably medieval or later 250 ⑤

Roman gold ring 253 ⑧

A Sites and Monuments Record comprises a description and assessment of known ancient monuments, a map showing the location of monuments and an archival record of the site - photographs, surveys and excavation reports.

FIGURE 6.8 Typical Uses of Article 4 Directions

Location	'Permitted development' rights restricted
Conservation Area	domestic works - extensions, porches, outbuildings, satellite dishes minor works - fences, walls, gates, accesses painting outside of buildings where appearance would be affected telecommunication equipment *Note some rights are automatically restricted in all Conservation Areas*
Countryside	agricultural development - buildings, alterations, excavations domestic works - extensions, porches, outbuildings, satellite dishes temporary uses of land for 14 or 28 days a year caravans exempt from other licensing camping by recreational organisations *Note some rights are automatically restricted in National Parks and Areas of Outstanding Natural Beauty*
Agricultural land	minor works - fences, walls, gates, accesses agricultural development - buildings, alterations, excavations *Note used to stop land being sub-divided and in especially attractive areas*
Houses	domestic works - extensions, porches, outbuildings, satellite dishes *Note where house or area is particularly high quality*
Nature conservation	temporary uses of land for 14 or 28 days a year *Note some temporary use rights are restricted automatically in Sites of Special Scientific Interest*

was made at Gartocharn in the Loch Lomond National Scenic Area to stop a 'rave' party taking place. A district council has to pay compensation to an applicant refused planning permission in these circumstances because he or she has been denied rights given by government automatically to everyone else.

Changes that have already taken place as well as 'permitted development' rights relating to mining, maintenance work by statutory undertakers and emergency works can't be included in an article 4 direction. Each article 4 direction specifies the type of 'permitted development' that is being restricted on a particular site, defined area or whole district. Article 4 directions, except those relating to Listed Buildings and some work in Conservation Areas, must have the government's prior approval before coming into effect. Article 4 directions relating to domestic development, fencing, painting, accesses, changes of use and temporary uses, come into effect as soon as they're made and last for only six months - unless the government confirms or rejects them in the meantime.

If development concerns you, you can find out if a site or area is covered by an article 4 direction by looking at the district council's Ordnance Survey maps at the planning department. The receptionist should be able to show you a copy of the direction documents and the accompanying plan and statement describing the area and the reasons why the article 4 direction was needed. If necessary ask a planning officer to explain the effect of the direction and draw his or her attention to the development that concerns you. The Local Plan might have some information on article 4 directions in the area. If you see development taking place, at one particular site or in a sensitive area of town or countryside, that's visually damaging or affecting character yet not covered by an article 4 direction, speak to a planning officer. An article 4 direction is one possible option available to the council to stop it or limit harm, by bringing the development under full planning control.

In this chapter we look at particular types of development which commonly cause concern or where special considerations apply. It's not to say that the categories mentioned are bad in themselves – indeed, they are all necessary. In each case we identify some of the considerations to bear in mind.

AGRICULTURAL DEVELOPMENT

The use of land or buildings for agricultural or forestry purposes isn't subject to normal planning control. Consequently, any land or buildings can be used for a purpose coming within the definition of 'agriculture' in planning law, which includes horticulture, market gardens, breeding and keeping any creature for the production of food, wool, skins or fur, and woodlands ancillary to farming. In addition to this general exemption from planning control, agricultural properties are given extensive 'permitted development' rights to put up and extend buildings, lay access tracks and carry out engineering works, without having to apply for planning permission. The siting and design of some types of agricultural 'permitted development' require prior approval by the council. Where harmful agricultural development takes place without planning permission, discuss with a planning officer whether permission was required or whether 'permitted development' rules have been complied with fully. The produce of an agricultural enterpise can also be sold off the farm so long as that retail element remains ancillary to the primary agricultrual use. This makes it difficult, for example, to distinguish at what point nurseries selling their produce become garden centres.

Agriculture enjoys special status in planning policies because it's one of the few uses deemed appropriate in the countryside. This can seem anomalous when industrial-type production methods taking place in industrial-type buildings, not dependent on the underlying soil or a rural location, are accepted on isloated green-field sites under council policies. Although more effort is made now to limit the impact of agricultural buildings and activities, planning officers and their councils still see agricultural development as largely beyond the normal planning criteria applied to most other forms of development. Noise, smells, vehicle movements, highway safety and appearance of buildings can all be valid objections to agricultural development. There might also be environmental health considerations so speak to that department of the council.

CAR REPAIRS

Although a very necessary use, it's nevertheless usually an unwelcome neighbour for a residential occupier. The nature of the business is such that it tends to pop up in virtually any small, and often poor-quality, building or in domestic garages or driveways. A very small-scale car-related business run from home, not involving much use of power tools, many comings and goings, noise or fumes, could be incidental to residential use and, therefore, not need permission. Some car-related activities that aren't especially disruptive, such as valeting or fitting car radios, could be classed as light industrial and so be capable of being accommodated in suitable buildings in or near residential areas. If the building concerned was already in light industrial or even office use, permission wouldn't be necessary. In the main, though, car repairs are classed as general industrial use which needs planning permission in any location outside an authorised industrial building. Get on to the council's planning or enforcement officer quickly if car repairs start up in a place you wouldn't normally expect or want them.

CARAVANS

There's no formal definition of 'caravan' or 'mobile home' in planning law. The one usually adopted is any structure or vehicle designed or adapted for human habitation capable of being moved under its own steam, by towing or on a trailer and two units, fixed together on site, normally qualify as long as they're under 60 x 20 x 10 feet high. Stationing a caravan is a use of land rather than a building operation and this has various implications. These include, first, that a caravan can be put on a site and used for the same purpose as the rest of the site, without permission. So, for example, a caravan can be placed on agricultural land and used for storage or by workers for shelter and refreshment (but couldn't be used as an independent dwelling). Second, the period within which councils can take enforcement action against the unauthorised stationing of a caravan is 10 years. Parking a caravan in the garden or drive of a house is ancillary to residential use and doesn't need permission. There are 'permitted development' rights to live in a caravan whilst working on a construction project, including building a single house, and for seasonal use of agricultural land as a caravan site for agricultural or forestry workers.

Special status is given to gypsies in planning policies, even though the same planning law and rules apply to gypsy caravans as they do to other caravans. Planning policies are supposed to cater for the needs of people with a nomadic lifestyle and local plans should identify suitable locations or criteria for transit and permanent sites which will normally be outside existing settlements yet with access to facilities. 'Gypsy' is defined as a person of nomadic habit of life regardless of race or origin. New age travellers are generally excluded and living permanently in one place can result in the loss of gypsy status. Apart from the residential use of gypsy sites, issues can arise from business uses on sites, such as scrap metal dealing and tarmac laying. Personal cicumstances are often a consideration in applications and enforcement cases, especially the need for schooling, and temporary permissions are sometimes used as a compromise. Travelling show people are not classed as gypsies although many similar considerations apply to sites for their winter quarters and seasonal permissions from November to April are often used.

EATING, DRINKING AND ENTERTAINMENT

Takeaways, amusement centres, discos, pubs and clubs can generate concerns over, among others, late-night disturbance and anti-social behaviour. Local plans often specify locations within town centres where these types of uses are allowed and situations where they're not, such as displacing shops in prime retail streets. Large-scale entertainment and leisure development is supposed to locate in town centres or, failing that, edge of centres or district centres before out-of-town positions are considered. Availability of public transport and/or parking is a factor. Amusement centres are normally restricted to secondary shopping and mixed commercial areas. Certain changes of use of premises can take place without planning permission because they fall within the same use class for planning purposes (see Figure 1.3), for example, cinema to bingo hall or pub to restaurant. Theatres are protected from this and any change of use needs permission. Activities, such as music, dancing or eating, can take place within other premises all the time they remain incidental to the primary function. This extends to computer or arcade games in takeaways, pubs or shops where the floor area used, number of machines or proportion of turnover determine whether that element is truly incidental, and many councils accept two machines as a rule of thumb.

One of the main fears with eating and entertainment uses is associated anti-social behaviour although, strictly speaking, unlawful activity isn't a planning issue but rather a matter for the police. However, noise inevitably created by people leaving a premises late at night – talking, slamming car doors and the thumping bass of car sound systems - is a legitimate planning issue. So too is noise eminating from the property itself and it's for these reasons that restrictions are usually put on opening hours. Councils often establish a standard closing time on noise-generating premises in a particular area. Cooking smells is another common concern which, in turn, can lead to objections to extraction and filtration plant and ducting, especially on listed buildings or in conservation areas.

FIGURE 7.1 Procedure for Approving a New Trunk Road

Programme	Government includes proposed new road in national Road Programme
Proposed routes	engineers identify possible routes; confidential consultation with official bodies
Public participation	alternative routes published for public comment
Preferred route	Government announces its chosen alternative
Draft orders	Government draws up and publishes road orders; environmental statement published, compulsory purchase order can be published at same time
Objections	owners of property affected and anyone else can write to relevant Government department objecting to road order
Public Inquiry arranged	Government notifies objectors of date and venue 6 weeks before public inquiry and sends statement of reasons for orders 4 weeks before inquiry; notice of inquiry published in newspapers and site notices put up 2 weeks before inquiry
Public Inquiry	independent inspector hears Government and objectors cases and reports to relevant Government department
Decision	relevant Government department considers report, confirms, modifies or rejects order; decision letter sent to objectors
Purchase	Government draws up associated side road orders and compulsory purchase orders to implement scheme

Potential harm from eating and entertainment uses can be reduced by planning conditions, for example requiring sound insulation, imposing noise limits, or restricting hours of use. Such uses are also covered by various licensing regimes including gaming, liquor and entertainment licences and each has its own separate criteria and restrictions.

HOSTELS AND RESIDENTIAL INSTITUTIONS

Hostel use, where care isn't provided, (homeless, ex-offenders, students) requires planning permission. Residential institution use, where care is provided, (rehabilitation, disabled, mentally ill) generally does too, although won't if the building was a nursing home, hospital or residential school or training centre. The definition of 'dwelling' includes up to six people living together as a household, even where care is provided, and so permission wouldn't be needed for a change of use from a family house to a residential institution use, providing all occupants, including carers, do live communally. There can be very fine distinctions between hotel, hostel, residential institution and dwelling uses.

Where permission is needed, decisions are supposed to be made on normal planning grounds, without taking into account the nature of occupants. The scale or intensity of local opposition and the fear of the behaviour of occupants aren't meant to be given over-riding weight. In practice, of course, councils are sensitive to public opinion which leads to a relatively large proportion of appeals being allowed for these types of proposal. However, some appeals have been refused partly because of wide-spread public concern and it's still something of a grey area. If you're opposing such an application, make sure you advance normal planning arguments (see Chapters 1 and 2) and try to collect evidence of the effects of similar developments elsewhere, but do also encourage as many people as possible to object and campaign with you.

HOUSEHOLDER DEVELOPMENT

This type of development refers to building work on or around an existing house and whilst projects can be small-scale, proximity to other houses often means such development seriously affects neighbours' enjoyment of their homes. Controlling or influencing householder development is complicated somewhat by the range of 'permitted development' rights which houses enjoy (see Figure 1.2). These enable quite large structures to be built close to adjoining houses, up against property boundaries or blocking views or light – all without planning permission. Having a good relationship with your neighbours is probably the best defence against potentially harmful building work. By the same token, if you're worried by neighbours' planning applications, it's worth trying to discuss your concerns with them before writing to the council as an objection might sour relationships.

The usual issues with householder development are loss of privacy, the new or resultant building appearing overbearing, loss of aspect, and loss of light. Most of these depend on window positions in the affected dwelling although the impact on gardens, especially private areas close to the house, should also be taken into account. The function of the rooms affected is important, with main living rooms and bedrooms being the most sensitive. Less weight is attached to the impact on a second window where a room has a main window in an unaffected elevation. The screening effect of planting trees or shrubs or fencing (a two-metre fence can be erected on a boundary without council permission) can be considered in weighing up a proposal. Loss of aspect isn't the same thing as loss of a particular view but concerns losing any outlook at all from a window – there are no rights to private views in planning. Similarly, whilst legal rights of light aren't a planning matter, in deciding planning applications councils should ensure habitable rooms would still receive adequate daylight and sunlight and often refer to Building Research Establishment guidelines for assessing daylight and sunlight.

HOUSING

Decisions on the amount and location of large-scale housing development are made through the plan-making process. Once a peice of land is allocated for such development in a Local Plan or Unitary Development Plan, it's almost inevitable the houses will be built and the only remaining questions to be resolved in a planning application are design, type, layout and number of units. Therefore, in order to influence housing development decisions, it's essential to make your voice heard during the Local Plan process (see Chapter 5).

One exception to this is so-called 'affordable housing'. This is housing generally owned or managed by 'social landlords', such as housing associations. If there's a proven need for low-cost housing in an area, and no sites are available inside a town or village, planning permission can be given outside defined policy boundaries where open-market housing wouldn't be allowed. Other planning standards – appropriate siting, access, design, layout and so on – are supposed to be met but councils sometimes regard this type of development as exempt from these as well.

NOISY COUNTRYSIDE ACTIVITIES

Shooting, motorbike scrambling, banger racing, model aircraft flying, paintball gaming and similar uses all generate intrusive noise, amongst other effects, such as threats to public safety, spoiling the enjoyment of the countryside for walkers and riders, scarring the landscape and harming wildlife. The principal issue with these uses is that 'permitted development' rights exist to use open land for any purpose for 28 days a year, and no more than 14 days can be for markets, car or motorbike uses. The rights don't apply to buildings or the grounds of a building, for example, land around a country house or in a building's car park. The number of days can only be used once at any one property or farm, which prevents more than the allowed number of activities taking place on different parts of a large landholding. War games, clay pigeon shoots and motor sports in SSSIs aren't permitted under this provision (see Chapter 6). As with other types of 'permitted development', councils can take away the rights in an article 4 direction (see Chapter 6). If you're affected by one of these uses you can ask the council to check that it's kept within the limitations, especially the number of days a year, and where it's particularly harmful, urge the officers or councillors to make an article 4 direction. Local authorities have the power to serve Noise Abatement Notices under other legislation and you can request the authority to use that power.

Use of land for such noisy activities beyond 28 or 14 days is subject to normal planning restrictions and the need for planning permission. Normal planning criteria must be taken into account including special designations (see Chapter 6), highway safety and adequacy and the appearance of related buildings, structures or hard surfacing. The impact of the uses can be mitigated by conditions on hours of use, number of days of use, noise levels, types of equipment or vehicles used and safety measures.

QUARRYING AND WASTE DISPOSAL

These uses are in some respects two sides of the same coin – minerals are dug out of the ground and transported away and the resultant hole is re-filled by waste material brought back in. Their impact is similar in terms of noise, vehcile movement and appearance. In each case planning decisions usually turn on the need, in the national interest, for minerals and for places to dispose of waste, weighed against environmental effects. Councils aim to maintain a supply of land with permission for these uses. Problems arise because minerals often lie under attractive countryside and most waste still goes into landfill despite moves to find alternatives. Also, waste is supposed to be deposited close to where it's generated. Quarrying and waste are dealt with by county councils, where this tier of local government exists, or otherwise by unitary councils. Typical issues are: landscape impact, noise of traffic and working on site, ground water pollution, dust and dirt, effect on public rights of way, loss of good agricultural land, smells and harm to wildlife and natural interest. Large scale proposals might require an environmental asessment (see page 33). Filling in the holes left by quarrying generally has less landscape impact than building up the ground level although worked out quarries can be important wildlife habitats or exhibit geological interest.

On a smaller scale, waste transfer operations can start up in scrap, haulage or storage yards instead of, or as well as, the pre-existing use. Waste transfer doesn't normally come into general industrial or storage use categories and planning permission is required for the use in addition to a waste licence.

ROADS

Trunk roads and motorways are government responsibilities which don't go through the normal planning application and appeals process but special orders are made giving the equivalent of planning permission. Public inquiries into these orders are generally similar to other inquiries (see Chapters 3 and 5) and provide an opportunity to influence the decision. Where compulsory purchase orders are also involved, this represents an additional opportunity. If the relevant orders aren't confirmed, road-building can't take place. Two main types of road order are made: a line order, which establishes a route; and a side road order, which deals with alterations needed to existing roads as a result of the proposed new road. It's often easier to challenge details of schemes rather than the principle so, before taking a proposal head on, think whether some amendment can make it acceptable to you. With road and compulsory purchase proposals you should object as strongly as possible, as early as possible. The farther a scheme gets, the harder it is to change so, in the case of trunk roads, mount a vigorous campaign at the public participation stage (see Figure 7.1).

Your objection can be made on normal planning grounds: environmental effect, visual impact, loss of historic buildings, effect on wildlife habitats and road safety. More technical highway objections can also be made and the government's representatives will produce traffic figures, forecasts and models showing the distribution and levels of vehicles using existing and proposed road networks. Such technical material is likely to be completely incomprehensible, certainly at first, and it's one area to think seriously about getting professional help. Your objection stands more chance of success if you can put forward an alternative road proposal. Co-operate with other objectors, clubbing together to get professional help and, if possible, by all arguing for the same alternative route or changes.

County councils and district councils deal with roads other than trunk roads and motorways and their road proposals are included in Structure and Local Plans. These roads must have planning permission and are publicised like other types of application.

Don't be put off objecting to a road proposal: it's a type of development like any other. The difference is that you've additional traffic grounds on which to oppose it.

TELECOMMUNICATIONS

The government strongly supports the extension of telecommunication services and, therefore, the masts, towers, dishes, antennas and associated equipment necessary to deliver those services. In the planning system this support takes two forms – wide powers to install telecommunication equipment without planning permisison and a permissive national planning policy.

There's a whole section of 'permitted development' rights devoted to telecommunications development and the rules are very detailed and complex. The most significant rights, only available to licensed telecommunication operators, include erecting ground-based masts up to 15 metres high (not in Scotland) and fixing masts of various heights up to 15 metres on buildings. There's also a general right to install a microwave antenna on a building over 15 metres high. Before putting up a mast under 'permitted development' rules, licensed telecommunication operators have to go through a prior approval procedure, involving an application to see whether the council wants to approve siting and design and putting up a site notice. The council then has eight weeks to make a decision and, unlike planning applications, if it doesn't, the project can go ahead. The only way a council can stop such a mast being built is by making an article 4 direction to take away the 'permitted development' right (see Chapter 6) but blanket directions covering wide areas aren't allowed. Apart from some government telecommunications installations, which are exempt from planning control, all masts outside the 'permitted development' rules require planning permission. Councils aren't supposed to question the need for the service, although applicants are supposed to show that they've investigated making use of existing masts as operators are expected to share facilities. Appearance and effect on the landscape are usually the main issues and the harm must be severe to overcome the policy of meeting the need for telecommunications services in the national interest. The effect of electro-magnetic radiation on health is another concern. Whilst the official view is that there's no harm, public fear of health risk has, in a few cases, led to planning refusals and appeals being dismissed. Attaching weight to public fear about unproven factors is a grey area in planning but the cases show that the more people who object, the more likely it is that permission will be refused.

WIND FARMS

The UK has one of the windiest climates in Europe and government's aim is to utilise this resource to generate 10% of the country's energy needs by the year 2025. It's unfortunate, then, that the highest winds in this country tend to blow across the most beautiful landscapes. The feasibility of wind turbines depends on average wind speeds, vehicle access and access to and capacity of the local electricity distribution network. These factors, together with the physical nature of the site, influence the number of turbines proposed and a large number of turbines are referred to as a 'wind farm'. A medium sized wind farm might have 10-25 turbines of 25-35 metre rotor diameter, the central hub of which would be about 30-35 metres high. Because the siting of wind turbines depends on variable factors, councils are supposed to give only broad guidance on appropriate locations in their Local Plans.

Landscape impact is usually a main issue in which the extent of public viewpoints and the fact that the movement of rotors draws the eye are factors. Visual impact, strobing or shadow flickering, electro-magnetic interference and noise, generated mechanically and by the rotor blades, are main issues for local residents. Once built, wind farms generate little traffic movement but it's recognised that motorists can be distracted by moving rotors.

Government guidelines say that wind turbine planning applications should include technical information such as colours and appearance, heights, rotor diameters, speed of rotation, wind speeds, projected noise levels and background noise levels.

Appendix I - Getting Professional Help

There's a great deal you can do by your own efforts to influence planning decisions. If you follow the steps set out in this book, your contribution could be effective because you will be putting relevant points to the people who matter, at the right time, and in the best way. What you can usefully achieve yourself depends on the time you're able to devote, on the scale and complexity of the planning case and on what forces are ranged against you. Major decisions that affect your life are taken through the planning system, which is constantly evolving. The professionals deal with the system every day and paying for their knowledge and experience can represent a valuable investment. In this Appendix we look at when and what help to get, and where to find it.

WHEN TO GET HELP

In theory, the planning system is open and accessible to members of the public, yet the reality can be quite different. To many people, Local Plans, public inquiries and planning procedures appear as a mass of jargon, form-filling and red tape. You might find help from someone who knows the ropes can save you a lot of headache, especially if the proposed development is large or complex. At no stage in the planning process, however, are you obliged to be professionally represented, but, if there's a great deal at stake, you might want to be sure everything possible is being done to protect your interests. This could be where:

- the value and enjoyment of your property is seriously affected by nearby development
- your health and safety are put at risk through increased traffic or pollution
- the future of your community is jeopardised by large-scale development
- your livelihood is threatened
- your home or business is threatened by re-development schemes

Specialist knowledge might prove invaluable when, for example, planning proposals concern a Site of Special Scientific Interest (see Chapter 6). Road layouts, traffic models, distribution and movements can be impenetrable to all but experienced highway engineers. Planning arguments can hinge on very fine points of legal interpretation, involving acts of Parliament, schedules, rules, orders, regulations and policy. Reams of conflicting statistics can be brought to bear by those supporting and objecting to a planning proposal. Use a professional to help with these complex and difficult areas.

If you're busy and don't have a great deal of time to spare, maybe having someone to do part or all of the work is the answer. Investigation, research, surveys and drawing up statements absorb considerable time to do properly and public inquiries can go on for days, weeks or months. Obviously, getting professional help costs money: fees range from about £50 an hour for a self-employed planning consultant to £200 or more an hour for a large national firm of planning consultants. Professional help could cost anything from a few hundred pounds for an objection to a planning application to tens of thousands of pounds for a full case to be presented at a public inquiry by a team of professionals. Campaigners against a lime stone quarry in Dyfed anticipated spending £30,000 on full representation at the public inquiry.

Always ensure you get a fee basis in writing for the advice before agreeing to go ahead. If you don't know of a consultant, perhaps speak to a few firms. Find out what experience they have and if you've any doubts, contact someone else they've acted for. Ask what they suggest should be done and how much they'll charge, and get this confirmed in writing. Fees could possibly be shared if you involve other people in your campaign. Contributing, say, £50 each is not a great deal, where a significant reduction in the value and enjoyment of your homes is at stake, and multiplied by 20 or 30 affected home-owners, could secure you professional representation and advice.

WHAT HELP TO SEEK

You can hand over to a consultant entirely or use him or her for a specific task such as supplying initial advice on a planning application. This might involve just one meeting or even a telephone call to talk about your concerns and get you started in the right direction. A good consultant can supply ideas on how to deal with particular issues, go through your letter of objection or statement, suggest a course of action and say what your chances of success are. He can also draw up a letter or statement, the length, detail and, therefore, cost depending on the nature of the proposal and how much you can afford to pay. Such a professional letter doesn't stop you lobbying councillors, turning up and speaking at an inquiry or even writing separately yourself. It might be worthwhile commissioning a report on the development proposal. The consultant can look into the case - speak to a planning officer, study the Local Plan, research planning history - and report on what chance the proposal stands, the issues involved and appropriate arguments to use.

Where specialist knowledge on, for example, architecture, highways, ecology or archaeology is important to a decision, choose an appropriately qualified consultant. If the prospect of public speaking at a formal inquiry and being cross-examined fills you with horror, you could appoint an advocate - planning consultant, solicitor or barrister - to deal with procedure and cross-examine witnesses. If you have an advocate you can still speak or, alternatively, use a planning consultant to act as an advocate and give the evidence. If you pass the whole case over to a planning consultant make sure you know at the outset what he's going to do. Ask to see drafts of statements before they're submitted and let him know how closely you want to stay in touch with the case.

WHERE TO FIND HELP

When selecting a consultant check that the person you contact is familiar with the complexities involved in your particular planned development. Figure 8.1 features some types of consultant who might be able to help you. In most cases the best person to seek assistance from is a planning consultant who is a chartered surveyor or town planner.

FIGURE 8.1 Types of Consultant

Consultant	Areas of expertise
Planning consultant (RICS or RTPI)	general planning advice, planning law and rules, applications, appeals, enforcement, Local Plans, public inquiries; can recommend barristers and other specialists
Highway engineer	new roads, road orders, road inquiries, traffic, highway safety, access
Landscape architect	visual assessment, National Parks, Areas of Outstanding Natural Beauty, countryside, landscape schemes
Solicitor	public inquiries, challenging decisions in courts, complex legal points
Barrister	public inquiries, court cases, complex legal points
Building surveyor	building designs, condition, repair, conversion and structure, Listed buildings, Conservation Areas
Architect	Listed buildings, Conservation Areas, building design
Environmental consultant	environmental assessment, pollution, nature conservation, visual assessment
Ecologist	wildlife, endangered species, pollution, nature conservation, planting and management schemes
Archaeologist	archaeological remains, Scheduled Ancient Monuments, Areas of Archaeological Importance, historic towns
Surveyor/estate agent	supply and demand for accommodation and land, market trends, occupation of property

Chartered surveyors are members of the Royal Institution of Chartered Surveyors (RICS) within which there is a specialist planning and development section. Some firms of surveyors have planning departments, other firms of surveyors work exclusively in planning consultancy. Chartered surveyors have a wide understanding of all aspects of property and development, beyond the planning system itself. They tend to have backgrounds in private practice consultancy and adopt a practical approach to property matters. Chartered town planners are members of the Royal Town Planning Institute (RTPI). Most chartered town planners work for councils or gain their initial practical experience working for local authorities before going into private practice. There are firms of chartered town planners and many other planning consultancies employ RTPI members.

People affected by proposed development often turn to their local solicitor. Generally speaking, solicitors' training and abilities are in the law and advocacy - not in assessing the planning merits of development proposals. There are, however, some solicitors who specialise in planning work. Planning solicitors can play a valuable role, particularly in enforcement cases and at inquiries, and can advise on a suitable barrister for the case and prepare the necessary brief. Some architects also offer specialist planning services. Most architects' skills lie primarily in the design of buildings rather than in planning consultancy. There are occasions where architecture is the main issue. In such cases an architect can provide specialist advice.

In certain areas, free planning advice is available to members of the public, and community and amenity groups through Planning Aid, a voluntary organisation sponsored by the RTPI. It can't give a full consultancy service but does offer guidance, for example, on whether to employ a consultant or how to deal with a problem yourself. Ask at your local council planning department about Planning Aid in your area.

As with other services, it's often best to find a planning consultant through personal recommendation. Ask your solicitor, surveyor, estate agent or other professional advisor. Your friends, colleagues or business associates might have used or know of a planning consultant. You still need to treat recommendations with a little caution because planning isn't a widely understood subject. Someone, for example, who is a good designer of house extensions might be well known locally but is probably not the best person to oppose, say, a commercial development in the Green Belt.

Contact local amenity groups to find out if they know of a consultant or, at a local library, look through professional directories or in Yellow Pages. The headquarters of the professional bodies (see Appendix II) will usually supply a list of suitable practices. If you are looking for consultants in a very specialist field, the professional bodies, or possibly the district council, are likely to be most informative.

Complaints

England

Greater London, Kent, Surrey, East Sussex and West Sussex:
Local Government Ombudsman
21 Queen Anne's Gate
London SWIH 9BU

East Anglia, the south-west, the west, the south and most of central England:
Local Government Ombudsman
The Oaks No 2, Westwood Way
Westwood Business Park
Coventry CV4 8JB

Cheshire, Derbyshire, Nottinghamshire, Lincolnshire and the north of England:
Local Government Ombudsman
Beverley House, 17 Shipton Road
York Y03 6FZ

Government Departments

Ombudsman for Northern Ireland
33 Wellington Place
Belfast BT1 6HN

Parliamentary Commissioner for Administration
Millbank Tower, Millbank
London SW1P 4QP

Inquiry Procedure

Council on Tribunals
22 Kingsway,
London WC2B 6LE

Northern Ireland

Parliamentary Ombudsman for Northern Ireland
33 Wellington Place
Belfast BT1 6HN

Scotland

Local Government Ombudsman
23 Walker Street
Edinburgh EH3 7HX

Wales

Local Government Ombudsman
Derwen House
Court Road
Bridgend
Mid Glamorgan CF31 1BN

Inspectors/Reporters/Commissioners

Chief Commissioner, Planning Appeals Commission
Park House, 87-91 Great Victoria Street
Belfast BT2 7AG
Tel: 028 9024 4710

Complaints Officer, The Planning Inspectorate
Temple Quay House, 2 The Square Street
Temple Quay
Bristol BS1 6PN
Tel: 0117 372 8000

Complaints Officer, The Planning Inspectorate
Crown Buildings, Cathays Park
Cardiff CF10 3NQ
Tel: 029 2082 3889

Unit Manager, Scottish Executive Inquiry Reporters Unit
2 Greenside Lane
Edinburgh EH1 3AG
Tel: 0131 244 5649

Government Advisory Bodies

Architecture/Historic Buildings

CABE: Commission for Architecture and the Built Environment
16th Floor The Tower Building,
11 York Road, London SE1 7NX
Tel: 020 7960 2400

CADW: Welsh Historic Monuments Executive Agency
Cathays Park, Cardiff CF10 3NQ
Tel: 029 2050 0200

Council for British Archaeology
Bowes Morrell House
111 Walmgate, York YO1 9WA
Tel: 01904 671417

English Heritage
23 Savile Row, London W1S 2ET
Tel: 0207 973 3000

Historic Scotland
Longmore House, Salisbury Place
Edinburgh EH9 1SH Tel: 0131 668 8600

Northern Ireland DoE, Environment and Heritage Service
5-33 Hill Street
Belfast BT1 2LA
Tel: 028 9023 5000

Royal Commission on Ancient and Historical Monuments of Scotland
John Sinclair House, 16 Bernard Terrace
Edinburgh EH8 9NX
Tel: 0131 662 1456

Royal Commission on Ancient and Historical Monuments in Wales
Crown Building, Plas Crug
Aberystwyth SY23 1NJ
Tel: 01970 621233

Royal Fine Arts Commission for Scotland
9 Atholl Crescent
Edinburgh EH3 8HA
Tel: 0131 229 1109

Countryside/Nature

Countryside Agency
John Dower House, Crescent Place
Cheltenham, Glos GL50 3RA
Tel: 01242 521381

Countryside Council for Wales
Plas Penrhos, Bangor
Gwynedd LL57 2LQ Tel: 01248 385500

English Nature
Northminster House, Northminster
Peterborough, Cambs PE1 1UA
Tel: 01733 455000

Northern Ireland DoE, Environment & Heritage Service
35 Castle Street, Belfast BT1 1GU
Tel: 028 9022 51477

Scottish Natural Heritage
12 Hope Terrace
Edinburgh EH9 2AS
Tel: 0131 447 4784

Requests to List Buildings

Listing Branch, CADW: Welsh Historic Monuments Executive Agency
Cathays Park, Cardiff CF1 3NQ
Tel: 029 2050 0200

Listing Branch, Department of Culture, Media and Sport
Trafalgar Place, 2-4 Cockspur Street
London SW1Y 5DH
Tel: 0270 211 6000

Listing Branch, Historic Scotland
Longmore House, Salisbury Place
Edinburgh EH9 1SH
Tel: 0131 668 8600

Northern Ireland DoE, Protecting Historic Buildings Branch
5-33 Hill Street, Belfast BT1 2LA
Tel: 028 9023 5000

Government Departments

Planning

Department of Transport, Local Government and the Regions
Eland House, Bressenden Place
London SW1E 5DU
Tel: 020 7944 3000 www.detr.gov.uk

National Assembly for Wales, Planning Division
Cathays Park, Cardiff CF1 3NQ
Tel: 029 2082 5111 www.wales.gov.uk

Northern Ireland DoE, Planning Service
Clarence Court, 10-18 Adelaide Street
Belfast BT2 8GB
Tel: 028 9054 0540 www.doeni.gov.uk

Planning Appeals Commission
Park House, 87-91 Great Victoria Street
Belfast BT2 7AG Tel: 028 9024 4710

Planning Inspectorate
Crown Buildings, Cathays Park
Cardiff CF10 3NQ Tel: 029 2082 3808

Planning Inspectorate
Temple Quay House, 2 The Square Street
Temple Quay, Bristol BS1 6PN
Tel: 0117 372 8000

Scottish Executive, Planning Division
Victoria Quay, Edinburgh EH6 6QQ
Tel: 0345 741741 www.scotland.gov.uk

Scottish Executive, Inquiry Reporters Unit
2 Greenside Lane, Edinburgh EH1 3AG
Tel: 0131 244 5680

Roads

Highways Agency
St Christopher House, Southwark Street
London SE1 0TE
Tel: 0845 955 6575

National Assembley for Wales, Transport Directorate
Crown Buildings, Cathays Park
Cardiff CF1 3NQ
Tel: 029 2082 5111

Northern Ireland DoE, Roads Service
4 Hospital Road
Hydebank
Belfast BT8 8JL
Tel: 028 9025 3000

Scottish Development Department
Victoria Quay
Edinburgh EH6 6QQ
Tel: 0131 556 8400

Professional Bodies

Archaeologists

The Institute of Field Archaeologists
The University of Reading
2 Earley Gate, PO Box 239
Reading, Berks RG6 6AU
Tel: 0118 931 6446

Architects

Royal Institute of British Architects
66 Portland Place
London W1B 1AD
Tel: 020 7580 5533

Ecologists

Institute of Ecology and Environmental Management
45 Southgate Street, Winchester
Hants SO23 9EH
Tel: 01962 868626

Environmental Consultants

Institute of Environmental Management and Assessment
St Nicholas House, 70 Newport
Lincoln LN1 3DP Tel: 01522 540069

Barristers

Bar Library, Royal Courts of Justice
Chichester Street, Belfast BT1 3JP
Tel: 028 9024 1523

Faculty of Advocates
Advocates Library, Parliament House
Edinburgh EH1 1RF
Tel: 0131 226 5071

Planning and Environment Bar Association
The Secretary, 2 Harcourt Buildings Temple
London EC4Y 9DB
Tel: 0171 353 8415

Building Surveyors

Royal Institution of Chartered Surveyors
12 Great George Street
London SW1P 3AD
Tel: 020 7222 7000

Highway Engineers

Institution of Civil Engineers
1 Great George Street, London SW1P 3AA
Tel: 020 7222 7722

Institution of Highways and Transportation
6 Endsleigh Street, London WC1H 0DZ
Tel: 0171 387 2525

Landscape Architects

Landscape Institute
6-8 Barnard Mews, London SW11 1QU
Tel: 020 7738 9166

Planning Consultants

Royal Institution of Chartered Surveyors
12 Great George Street, London SW1P 3AD
Tel: 020 7222 7000

Royal Town Planning Institute
26 Portland Place, London W1N 4BE
Tel: 020 7636 9107

Solicitors

Law Society
113 Chancery Lane, London WC2A 1PL
Tel: 020 7242 1222

Law Society of Northern Ireland
98 Victoria Street, Belfast BT1 3JZ
Tel: 028 9023 1614

Law Society of Scotland
26 Drumsheugh Gardens
Edinburgh EH3 7YR
Tel: 0131 226 7411

Surveyors/Estate Agents

Royal Institution of Chartered Surveyors
12 Great George Street
London SW1P 3AD
Tel: 020 7222 7000

Other Organisations

Agricultural

Farmers Union of Wales
Llys Amaeth, Plas Gogerddan, Aberystwyth
Dyfed SY23 3BI Tel: 01970 820820

National Farmers Union
Agriculture House, 164 Shaftesbury Avenue
London WC2H 8HL Tel: 020 7331 7200

National Farmers Union of Scotland
Rural Centre, West Mains, Ingliston
Mid Lothian EH28 8LT Tel: 0131 472 4000

Ulster Farmers Union
475 Antrim Road, Belfast BT15 3DA
Tel: 028 9037 0222

Appeal Decision Service

Development Control Services Limited
Suite 1, 40 Lower Quay Street
Gloucester GL1 2LW   Tel: 01452 310566

Commercial Development

Chamber of Commerce -
see Yellow Pages directories

Countryside/Nature

Association for the Protection of Rural
Scotland
Gladstone Land, 3rd Floor
483 Lawnmarket, Edinburgh EH1 2NT
Tel: 0131 225 7013

Campaign for the Protection of Rural Wales
Ty Gwyn, 31 High Street, Welshpool
Powys SY21 7YD Tel: 01938 552525

Council for the Protection of Rural England
Warwick House
25 Buckingham Palace Road, London SW1W 0PP
Tel: 020 7976 6433

National Trust
36 Queen Anne's Gate, London SW1H 9AS
Tel: 020 7222 9251

National Trust for Scotland
28 Charlotte Square , Edinburgh EH2 4ET
Tel: 0131 226 5922

National Trust (Northern Ireland)
Rowallane House, Saint Field, Ballynahinch
Co Down BT24 7LH   Tel: 028 9051 0721

Royal Forestry Society of England
Wales and Northern Ireland
102 High Street, Tring, Herts HP23 4AF
Tel: 01442 822028

Royal Society for Nature Conservation
(Wildlife Trust)
The Kiln, Waterside, Mather Road, Newark
Notts NG24 1WT
Tel: 01636 670000

Royal Society for the Protection of Birds
The Lodge, Sandy, Bedfordshire SG19 2DL
Tel: 01767 680551

Ulster Society for the Preservation of the
Countryside
2a Windsor Road, Belfast BT9 7FQ
Tel: 028 9038 1304

Wildlife and Countryside Link
89 Albert Embankment, London SWE1 7TP
Tel: 020 7820 8600

Wildlife Trusts - see Yellow Pages directories

Environment

Friends of the Earth
26 Underwood Street
London N1 7JT
Tel: 020 7490 1555

Greenpeace (UK)
Canonbury Villas
London N1 2PN
Tel: 020 7865 8100

Historic Buildings, Conservation Areas and Archaeology

Ancient Monuments Society
St Anns Vestry Hall, 2 Church Entry
London EC4V 5HB   Tel: 020 7236 3934

Belfast Civic Trust
28 Bedford Street, Belfast BT2 7SE
Tel: 028 9023 8437

Civic Trust (England and Wales)
17 Carlton House Terrace, London SW1Y 5AW
Tel: 020 7930 0914

Georgian Group
6 Fitzroy Square, London W1P 5DX
Tel: 020 7387 1720

National Trust
36 Queen Anne's Gate, London SW1H 9AS
Tel: 020 7222 9251

National Trust for Scotland
28 Charlotte Square, Edinburgh EH2 4ET
Tel: 0131 243 9300

National Trust (Northern Ireland)
Rowallane House, Saint Field, Ballynahinch
Co Down BT24 7LH
Tel: 028 9751 0721

Rescue: The British Archaeological Trust
15A Bull Plain, Hertford, Herts SG14 1DX
Tel: 01992 553377

SAVE Britain's Heritage
70 Cowcross Street, London EC1M 6EJ
Tel: 020 7253 3500

Scottish Civic Trust
The Tobacco Merchants House
42 Miller Street, Glasgow G1 1DT
Tel: 0141 221 1466

Society for the Protection of Ancient Buildings
37 Spital Square, London E1 6DY
Tel: 020 7377 1644

Twentieth Century Society
70 Cowcross Street, London EC1M 6EJ
Tel: 020 7250 3857

United Kingdom Association of Building
Preservation Trusts
Clareville House, 26-27 Oxendon Street
London SW1Y 4EL Tel: 020 7930 1629

Victorian Society
1 Priory Gardens, Bedford Park
London W4 1TT
Tel: 020 8944 1019

Noise

Noise Abatement Society
44 Grand Parade, Brighton BN2 2QA

Open Spaces, Recreation and Common Land

Garden History Society
70 Cowcross Street, London EC1M 6EJ
Tel: 020 7608 2409

National Playing Fields Association
Stanley House, St Chad's Place
London WC1X 9HH Tel: 020 7833 5360

Open Spaces Society
25A Bell Street, Henley-on-Thames
Oxon RG9 2BA
Tel: 01491 573535

Rights of Way and Footpaths

Open Spaces Society
25A Bell Street, Henley-on-Thames
Oxon RG9 2BA
Tel: 01491 573535

Ramblers Association
2nd Floor Camelford House, 87-89 Albert
Embankment, London SE1 7TW
Tel: 020 7339 8500

Roads

Transport 2000
The Impact Centre, 12-18 Hoxton Street
London N1 6NG Tel: 020 7613 0743

The Impact Centre
12-18 Hoxton Street, London N1 6NG
Tel: 020 7613 0743

Waterway

Environment Agency (England and Wales) -
see telephone directory

Inland Waterways Association
Po Box 114, Ricksmansworth
Herts WD3 1ZY
Tel: 01923 711114

Rivers Purification Boards (Scotland) - see
telephone directory

Water Service Northern Ireland DoE - see
telephone directory

DTLR Free Literature
PO Box 236 Wetherby, West Yorks LS23
7NB Tel: 0870 122 6236

- Compulsory purchase orders guide
- Cost awards in planning appeals
- Compulsory purchase order guide
- Enforcement notice appeals
- Environmental assessment
- Land compensation: your rights explained (series of five booklets)
- Local plans and unitary development plans
- Outdoor advertisements and signs
- Planning: a guide for householders
- Planning permission a guide to business
- Public inquiries into road proposals

Planning Inspectorate
Temple Quay House
2 The Square Street, Temple Quay
Bristol BS1 6PN
Tel: 0117 372 8000

- Guide to taking part in planning appeals
- Making your planning appeal

Scottish Executive Planning Division
Planning Services, Victoria Quay
Edinburgh EH6 6QQ
Tel: 0345 741741

- Guide to the planning system in Scotland
- Planning charter standard statement

Scottish Executive Inquiry Reporters Unit
2 Greenside Lane
Edinburgh EH1 3AG
Tel: 0131 244 5680

- Planning permission appeals in Scotland

Town and Country Planning Service
Northern Ireland DoE
Clarence Court, 10-18 Adelaide Street
Belfast BT2 8GB
Tel: 028 9054 0540

- Commenting on a planning application
- Environmental assessment
- Making a complaint on planning matters
- Planning application pack
- Tree preservation orders
- Your permitted development rights and environmental assessment

Appendix III - Glossary

Advance Notice of Decision
indication of the result of an appeal inquiry given before the formal decision is issued

adverse objection
objection to a Local Plan made to change it in a way that would be against your interests

agent
any representative who acts for an applicant for planning permission, appellant or Local Plan objector

AONB
see Area of Outstanding Natural Beauty

appeal questionnaire
standard form completed by a district council giving details of an appeal that is sent to the Planning Inspectorate and appellant

appeal statement
written case in support of, or opposing, an appeal that is considered by a planning inspector

appellant
an applicant for planning permission who appeals against the council's decision

appropriate development
limited types of development that are allowed in Green Belts: agriculture, outdoor sports, cemeteries, limited infilling, re-use of existing buildings

applicant
individual or body that applies for planning permission

Area of Archaeological Importance
historic area designated to protect archaeological remains where proposed ground works must be notified to the council

Area of Outstanding Natural Beauty
defined area of countryside formally designated to protect its scenic value

breach of planning control
development carried out without planning permission or without complying with conditions on a planning permission

Building Preservation Notice
notice served by a council giving emergency protection to a building while the Secretary of State decides whether to list the building

called-in application
planning application where the Secretary of State takes responsibility for making the decision from the council

closing speech
summing up of a case at an inquiry by each party's advocate

commissioner
see Planning Appeals Commission

compulsory purchase order
documents showing the land to be bought by an authority, the purpose for which the land is being bought and who owns each part of the land covered

cross-examine
asking witnesses questions at a public inquiry about their cases

decision letter
letter sent to appellant, council and others by a planning inspector giving the result of an appeal and reasons for the decision

decision notice
document setting out the result of a planning application sent to an applicant by the council

delegated decision
decision of a planing application taken by a planning officer on behalf of the council

deferred decision
decision of a planning committee to put off deciding a planning application pending further information or action

deposit draft Local Plan
formal stage in drawing up a Local Plan when it is published and objections and representations can be made

deposit period
time allowed to make formal objections and representations on a draft Local Plan of at least six weeks

DTLR

Department of Transport, Local Government and the Regions

developer

individual or body that carries out development but usually used to describe those who develop for profit rather than for their own use or occupation

development control officer

planning officer dealing with planning applications and appeals as opposed to Local Plans

development plan

formal title for the Structure and Local Plan, or the Unitary Development Plan

district council

local government responsible for a district within a county dealing with most day to day planning matters including planning applications (used in this book to include city and borough councils and unitary authorities)

enforcement

collective term for council's powers to deal with unauthorised development

enforcement officer

council officer responsible for investigating unauthorised development and complaints about development made by the public

environmental assessment

detailed statement required in a limited number of cases on the effects a proposed development would have on the environment that is assessed by a council or inspector in reaching a decision

evidence

facts and opinion put forward by a witness at an inquiry in support of a case

full planning permission

consent to carry out development that includes all details of buildings, layout, access and alterations

Green Belt

land around certain major towns and cities formally designated to stop urban sprawl and protect countryside

informal hearing

procedure for deciding planning appeals where an inspector leads a discussion about the main issues between the appellant and council

Inquiry Reporters Unit

body that administers the work of inquiry reporters who decide and report on planning appeals and Local Plans in Scotland

Inquiry inspector

see Planning Inspectorate

landscape officer

council officer responsible for trees, tree planting schemes and landscape matters

Lawful Development Certificate (LDC)

document issued by a council stating that planning permission is not needed for the development specified in the application

line order

document approving the route or centre line of a proposed section of trunk road

Listed Buildings

buildings and structures recorded in a statutory list given additional protection because of their special historic or architectural value

Local Plan

document comprising maps and a written statement setting out a council's policies for new development and controlling development in its area

local planning authority

council with responsibility for planning matters

major development

types of large scale development for which planning applications must be advertised in a local newspaper

material considerations

factors which should be taken into account in making planning decisions, such as government advice, special designations and the nature of the site and its surrounding area

Minerals Plan

council's planning policy document for exploration, extraction and treatment of minerals

minor development

types of small scale development for which planning applications do not have to be advertised in local newspapers

National Park

specially protected area of attractive countryside, with its own authority dealing with planning, designated to preserve and enhance its natural beauty and to promote its enjoyment by the public

National Planning Guidelines (NPGs)

statements of government planning policy for Scotland each covering a particular topic

National Scenic Area

area of attractive countryside in Scotland formally designated to protect its scenic value

neighbour notification

letter sent to people near a site letting them know that a planning application has been made

outline planning permission

consent to carry out development in principle with some or all of the details left to be established later, cannot be given for changes of use, engineering works or mining

parish council

local government body covering a parish within a district, made up of elected councillors who have no legal powers to decide planning applications but often have influence with the district council (used in this book to include town and community councils)

permitted development

types of development given planning permission automatically by a central government order which removes the need to apply for a planning permission

Planning Advice Note

statement of government planning policy for Scotland covering a particular topic

planning agreement

see planning obligation

Planning Appeals Commission

body that administers the work of commissioners who decide and report on planning appeals and Local Plans in Northern Ireland

planning application

application made to a council for permission to carry out building work and changes of use of buildings and land; comprises forms, location plan, plans and drawings, certificate of land ownership and council's fee

planning consultant

professional who advises clients on development proposals and planning law, procedure and practice

planning gain

benefit provided for the public by applicant as part of a planning permission, such as road improvements or community buildings

Planning Inspectorate

body that administers the work of planning inspectors who decide and report on planning appeals and Local Plans in England and Wales

planning obligation

legal document signed by a landowner, usually in connection with a planning application, requiring him to carry out or contribute towards the cost of specified work or to limit the use of land and buildings

planning officer

local government employee who carries out the work and implements the policies of the council, gives technical advice to council committees and information to members of the public

Planning Policy Guidance Notes

statements of government planning policy for England each covering a particular topic

programme officer

person employed by a district council to administer a Local Plan inquiry and liaise between the inspector, planning officers and objectors

proposals map

plan showing the area covered by a Local Plan indicating where various policies apply and identifying sites allocated for development

public inquiry
formal hearing open to the public where cases for and against a development proposal are made and examined by an inspector

re-examine
further questions put by parties' advocates to their own witnesses after cross-examination

Regional Planning Guidance Notes
statements of government planning policy for the regions of England covering a broad strategy for development

reserved matters application
application made to a council for the approval of details of siting, layout, design, access and landscaping after outline planning permission has been given

road order
see line order and side road order

Scheduled Ancient Monument
archaeological remains or structure included in a statutory schedule, given additional protection because of its national importance

section 106 agreement
see planning obligation

side road order
document approving changes to existing roads and junctions needed as a result of a new section of trunk road

site notice
formal notice put up on a property to publicise a planning application or public inquiry

Site of Special Scientific Interest
area formally designated to protect its particular wildlife or geological features

SSSI
see Site of Special Scientific Interest

statutory plan
Structure or Local Plan or Unitary Development Plan that has completed the formal plan-making process and is then given special status in planning decisions

Structure Plan
written document with a key diagram setting out the council's broad development strategy and planning policies for its county or region

Technical Advice Notes (TAN)
statements of government planning policy for Wales covering a particular topic

TPO
see Tree Preservation Order

Tree Preservation Order (TPO)
document identifying single trees, groups, areas or woodlands that are protected from any work or felling without permission

Unitary Development Plan
planning policy document in areas with single-tier councils fulfilling the functions of a Structure and Local Plan

Urban Development Corporations
bodies set up to help regenerate derelict areas of certain cities, now disbanded

Waste Plan
council's planning policy document covering land filling, amenity tips, waste transfer and processing waste

Index

A

Abbey House Hotel, Barrow-in-Furness, 124

access and parking, 27, 34

Action Group for the Preservation of Village Life, 47

adverse objections, 97

"affordable" housing, 134

agent, 26

amusement centres, 131

appeal decision letter, 75-7

appeal form, 59-64

appeal plan, 68

appeal statements, 60, 65-70
    enforcement, 87-8

appellants, 60, 65, 66, 70-5

applicant, 9, 21, 22, 26, 35, 37

application forms, 23-8, 32

archaeological sites, 124-5

archaeologists, 140

architects, 140, 141

Areas of Archaeological Importance (AAIs), 125

Areas of Outstanding Natural Beauty (AONBs), 12, 13, 42, 45, 114-7

article 4 directions, 125, 127-8

B

Biogenetic Reserve, 118

borough and city councils, 8, 9
    see also district councils

breach of condition notice, 86

Brecon Beacons National Park, 113

British Nuclear Fuels, 113

the Broads, 12, 13, 112, 114-5

Brunswick Town Conservation Area (Hove), 120

Building Preservation Notice, 122

building near houses, 18

built environment and conservation, 91

Bungay Castle (Suffolk), 125

C

CADW (Welsh Historic Monuments Executive Agency), 52, 122

call-in, 52, 54, 107-8

Campaign for Real Ale, 50

Canterbury AAI, 125

changes of use, 14

Chester AAI, 125

Chief Commissioner/Reporter, 77

Citizens Advice Bureaux (CABs), 20, 80

community services, 91

compensation, 84, 85, 86

compulsory purchase, 135-6

compulsory purchase orders, 132, 135-6

Conservation Area consent, 17, 119

Conservation Areas, 12, 13, 42, 45, 91, 110, 119-21
    article 4 directions, 125, 127-8
    demolition, 84, 119
    Listed Buildings, 119
    trees, 110, 119

consultation draft, 90, 94, 97, 98

consultees, 21, 50-2, 94

Cotswold District, 119

Council on Tribunals, 77

Council for the Protection of Rural England, 49, 117

councillors, 15, 39, 41, 50, 81-2, 93-4

Countryside Agency, 112-3

Countryside Council for Wales, 52, 112-3, 118

county councils, 8-9, 10, 50, 90, 124, 136

D

deferred decisions, 55

delegated decisions, 55

deposit drafts, 90, 92, 94, 98

Department of Transport, Local Government and the Regions, 10, 52, 54, 107-8, 132

developers, 9, 81, 89, 97

development, 9, 27
    without planning permission, 9, 12-3, 79-88

discos, 131

district councils (including city and borough councils), 8-11, 17, 20-3, 36, 50, 81, 116-117, 121-2, 124, 125
    appeals, 58-78
    Local Plans, 89-108
    planning committee, 21
    planning department personnel, 36
    road building and compulsory purchase, 136
    unauthorised developments, 79-88

Divisional Planning Office/Officer, 8, 10, 21, 39, 55

drainage, 28

Dyfed limestone quarrying, 139

E

ecologists, 140

pressure groups, 49-50

procedural complaints, 77, 108

professional help, 138-41, 160

programme officer, 102, 104

public inquiries, 58-9, 71-5,
104-6, 139
into Center Parc plan, 54,
117
Local Plans, 104-6
planning appeals, 71-5
road and compulsory
purchase orders, 132
seating plan and duties of
involved parties, 72
speaking at, 73-5

public libraries, 20, 45, 92,
118, 141

public rights of way, 32

R

radio and TV, local, 49

Ramblers Association, 50

Ramsar Site, 118

recreation, tourism and leisure,
91

reference number, appeal, 60
planning application, 26, 59

reserved matters application, 26-7

road building and compulsory
purchase, 135-6
road orders, 132, 135-6
objection to, 132
line, 135-6
side, 135-6

Rochdale, quarry, 7

Royal Institution of Chartered
Surveyors (RICS), 140, 141

Royal Society for the
Protection of Birds, 50

Royal Town Planning Institute,
140, 141

S

Scheduled Ancient
Monuments, 84, 124-5

Scottish Natural Heritage, 52,
112, 118

Scottish Nuclear, 54

Scottish planning system, 6-7,
8, 10, 11, 16, 20, 52, 58,
71, 75, 89, 112, 118, 121,
122, 123, 124

Secretary of State for Culture,
Media and Sport, 121, 124

Scottish Executive, 10, 48, 52,
54, 110, 124

Secretary of State for the
Environment, Transport and
the Regions, 10, 52, 80

Section 215 notice, 86

Sherington, Bucks, 7

Shrewsbury and Atcham TPO,
110

side road orders, 132, 135-6

sites, 42, 46
address, 27
area, 27
existing uses, 28
inspecting, 34, 35
inspector's visit to, 66, 70,
71, 75, 106
notices, 20, 22, 48, 59
photographs, 35, 68, 69
trees on, 28

Sites and Monuments Record,
124-5, 126

Sites of Special Scientific
Interest (SSSI), 42, 117-9,
138
additional nature
conservation designations
applying to, 118

solicitors and barristers, 73,
105, 139, 140, 141

Special Area of Conservation,
118

special designations, 11, 12,
42, 45, 109-28

Special Protection Area, 118

stop notice, 85, 86

Structure Plans, 9, 10, 11, 69,
89, 103, 110, 113, 116-7

surrounding area, 43

surveyors, chartered, 140, 141
building, 140

T

Takeaways, 131

Tarleton horticulture, 85

Technical Advice Notes, 11, 17

technical consultees, 94

temporary buildings and uses,
13, 134-5

Tommy Ducks pub,
Manchester, 50

town councils, 9

town planners, 141

traffic, 135-6
vehicle counts, 68

Tree Preservation Orders
(TPOs), 28, 42, 45, 84,
109-10, 111

trespass, 80

trunk roads, 135-6

U

Unitary Development Plan, 9,
10-11, 89

'unreasonable behaviour', 73

utilities, public, 91, 94

V

Victorian Society, 50

W

Walton on Thames
development, 50

Wansbeck District Local Plan,
102

Waste Plans, 10, 90

Welsh Assembly, 48, 52, 54,
110, 124

Wildlife Trust, 118

written representation appeals,
58-9, 65-70

Y

York AAI, 125

Dear Reader

We hope you find HOW TO STOP AND INFLUENCE PLANNING PERMISSION as useful as do the many people who have contacted us since the first edition was published in 1994, and received such a positive reaction. Some parish councils bought four or five copies for their councillors, organisations recommended it enthusiastically in their magazines and newsletters to their members, individuals contacted us to tell us how it had helped them and people wrote to us with their own stories of how they had battled in the planning system. This was all extremely gratifying because it told us we had succeeded in our objective - to empower people to make their views count in the planning system.

However, most readers who contacted us did so because, having read our book, they wanted to find out if we were able to help them on a professional basis, by giving them specific advice on their particular problem or issue, or by representing them. Needless to say, as practising planning consultants, experienced in stopping and influencing planning decisions, working with or on behalf of groups and individuals, we are pleased to do this where we can. Some readers just needed a review of the relevant documents and direction for them or their campaign. Others asked us to research and report to them on a proposed development and what arguments to use against it. Many invited us to take on a case for them - fighting applications, appeals and inquiries. Not only have we been able to help readers throughout the country but the experience gained has been fed back into this revision of the book.

So, where you, your group or your parish council, need professional assistance, you are welcome to get in contact with us. Telephone numbers and an address are given on the next page. Also, if you have run or participated in a campaign to stop or influence development, please write to us about it so that we can feature your story in the future.

We wish you success with your participation in the planning system.

Roy Speer   *Michael Dade*

Roy Speer   *Michael Dade*

Roy Speer and Michael Dade are
consultants, writers and speakers, and
leaders in the field of helping people to
understand planning and have an
effective voice in the system. Both are
chartered surveyors with degrees in
Estate Management. They run their own
specialist town and country planning
practice, carrying out work in all parts of
the country for individuals, interest and
community groups, parish councils,
businesses and other organisations.

Their consultancy work includes
advising on planning applications,
appeals and enforcement, giving
evidence at hearings and public
inquiries, researching and reporting on
development proposals. In response to
readers' requests, they also provide a
useful and cost-effective advice-by-post
service.

Roy Speer and **Michael Dade**
can be contacted on:
01273 843737 or 01825 890870

roy@stonepound.co.uk
mike@stonepound.co.uk

c/o **Stonepound Books,**
10 Stonepound Road,
Hassocks, West Sussex BN6 8PP